The NEW
Caravan
and Motor Home
Handbook

John Marchmont

PRACTICAL GUIDE
to the OPEN ROAD

BookEns

i

First published in 2010 by BookEns, Royston, Hertfordshire

ISBN 978-0-9540692-3-0

Although the number of female caravanners is roughly equal to the number of males, the male pronoun has largely been used throughout this book. This avoids ponderous phraseology, and no discrimination or prejudice is intended.

Whilst this book has been compiled with the assistance of the National Caravan Council, the views expressed in it are those of the author.

Typeset by BookEns Ltd, Royston, Herts

Printed by Replika Press, India

Contents

Acknowledgement

I am, as always, deeply indebted to the Technical Staff of the National Caravan Council and several staff members of both the Caravan Club and the Camping and Caravan Club, all of whom have devoted valuable time in helping me to ensure the continued accuracy of the book. I also owe much to the various caravan publications whose information and material I have plundered shamelessly.

Much of the material in the following pages is particularly relevant to what today would be considered out of date, elderly caravans. We include bits of DIY which today's van manufactures have taken on board and now include as standard features.

I make no apology, therefore, for the occasional reference to vans with many miles on the clock with DIY features which owners of modern vans already enjoy.

This book is aimed at vans of all vintages since there is still a great number of vans twenty five and more years old, and still giving good service. Their financial value is negligible and so tend to be in the hands of newcomers to the hobby at the beginning of the learning curve.

I hope these jottings may be of some help to them.

I am grateful to the various accessory manufacturers who have readily provided information, and in many cases, samples of their products. Also, to those who have taken advertising space in the book.

Last, but certainly not least, my thanks to my wife *(Herself)* for her unfailing encouragement and help, and for the pleasure of her company on so many caravanning expeditions.

John Marchmont
January 2010

First Thoughts

The numerical gap between caravans and motor homes is rapidly closing and because much of the material in the following pages applies equally to both caravans and motor homes you will frequently see the word 'vans', in which case the subject covered will apply to both types of 'recreational vehicles' unless we say otherwise. Specifying 'caravans and motor homes' several time per page would just be tedious repetition.

As technology develops it is true to say that present day vans, while not actually complicated are certainly complex and to illustrate this let me cite the case of Grove Products Ltd. Grove Products are the principal wholesalers to the caravan trade, and their current catalogue lists over four thousand separate items; everything in fact from a 12 volt light bulb to a complete air conditioning unit.

Among the 4,000 items they supply are no doubt identical and equally effective items of equipment which are described, with a brand name, in the following chapters, and all these branded items, or something very similar, are available from caravan and/or motor home dealers.

Foreword

Welcome to caravanning. The start of a journey of freedom, of adventures, of new places to discover and well-loved destinations to enjoy.

Caravanning is certainly popular. The British Caravan Industry is now the second largest in the world, having overtaken both Germany and Holland this year. Only the US market is bigger.

All those new caravans means lots of new caravanners, and those new caravanners need several things to get the full value from their new purchase.

First of all, they need knowledge... information... advice... they need experience.

The Americans have a really good saying: "Experience only starts when you begin". So get out there, and start enjoying your caravan. You'll find that learning can be fun.

But you will also want some good advice, and you will find that John Marchmont's Caravanner's Handbook is full of it.

John is ready to share his years of experience with you and, in the pages of the book, you can learn from his decades of caravanning and even from his mistakes.

The other thing a new caravanner will need is some accessories. John's got some good advice on those too. What you need and, even more important, what you can do without.

I don't agree with John on everything. Some ten years ago, I road-tested an imported German caravan - the Knaus Sudwind. It had, what at that time, was a unique feature. A fixed double bed with a one piece mattress. Not one made up of smaller cushions.

My wife Ann and I loved it. And I wrote campaigning articles suggesting the British industry should take up this wonderful Continental idea. British caravan designers, to a man - and sadly they nearly all are men - told me I was foolish. Fixed double beds would never catch on.

Today, every British manufacturer sells models with a fixed double bed. They are popular, but still not popular with the author of this handbook. But it is differences of opinion like this that make for interesting discussion on campsites with a glass of wine in your hand.

The last thing a new caravanner is going to need is somewhere to use their caravan - a pitch on a campsite. Clubs, like my own, The Camping and Caravanning Club, offer hundreds of sites and information on thousands more. No wonder John makes a really good case for joining a Club in this book.

For one hundred and eight years, The Camping and Caravanning Club has provided its members with all sorts of services. Today, we have four hundred thousand members and we are growing fast. That illustrates, not just the success of the Club, but the popularity of caravanning. The freedom, the choice of leisure breaks - a great way to use your spare time.

Welcome to the great world of caravans. This book is certainly a great place to start your journey.

Peter

Peter Frost
Chairman, The Caravan Writers Guild
Formerly Director of Communications
The Camping and Caravanning Club

Preface

Like many others, I used to be 'anti-caravans', not only when they were on the road but on the various caravan parks up and down the country. I then read an earlier edition of The Caravanner's Handbook by John Marchmont and thoroughly enjoyed the contents. It certainly changes my views, and in fact the IAM now conducts an Advanced Caravan Towing test for its members.

The new edition is now fully up to date and is written in a lighthearted but informative way. It will help the novice caravanner to take up caravanning successfully and enjoy the freedom of taking part of your home with you.

There are excellent chapters on the actual towing procedure, reversing and manoeuvring and general hints. You will also find useful sections on camping sites in the UK and in Europe, and on motor homes, as well as a whole range of other important topics.

This book will certainly assist and improve your towing skills, making you a safe and considerate caravanner and so creating a better relationship between the car driver and the caravanner.

Ted Clements MBE
Former Chief Examiner Institute of Advanced Motorists

Bailey: Caravans
Bristol Fashion

CELEBRATING
60
YEARS
1948–2008

FOR HOMES
OR
HOLIDAYS

BAILEY

Sixty Years of Innovation

Founded in 1948 Bailey Caravans is the longest established UK independent manufacturer with nearly sixty years experience in caravan design and production. During this period it has grown to become the UK's number one caravan brand and now accounts for approximately one in three new caravan sales.

But what makes our caravans so popular and what makes them unique? The answer lies in a company culture where **production efficiency, technical excellence** and **design innovation** remain central to our thinking.

To find out how these concepts work in real terms and to give an insight in to what it takes to manufacture caravans "Bristol fashion" please visit our web site @
www.bailey-caravans.co.uk/info/profile.htm

Images courtesy of The Caravan Club and Alan Bond Photography.

Choosing
a Caravan
and a suitable tow car

▶ **General Guide to Selection**

▶ **The Towcar**
Weight and engine size of car

▶ **Accommodation and Size**
*Sleeping, cooking and
dining, Awning*

▶ **Trailer Tents and Folding Campers**

▶ **Caravan Construction**
*Chassis
Windows
Internal features
Additions and modifications
Second-hand caravans*

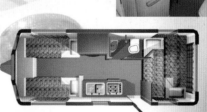

Where do you start?

What you decide to go for usually depends on two factors
(1) How many people it must accommodate *and*
(2) what you can afford.

Have you got a particular make in mind, or haven't you got that far yet? If you include imported caravans there are over two dozen makes to consider.

The following are UK made and either belong to two principal groups or are independent.

Caravans vary quite considerably for example they can be:-

Compact

Curiosity

Conventional

Commmodious

The independents are:		
Bailey	Lunar	Coachman
Vanmaster		
The Explorer Group include:		
Buccaneer	Compass	Elddis
The Swift Group include:		
Abbey	Swift	Ace
Sterling	Sprite	

owned by Adria, a Slovenian company

Compact

The NEW complete Caravan and Motor Home *Handbook*

Curiosity

Conventional

Commodious

Choosing a Caravan and a suitable tow car

Every caravan manufacturer, if you look closely, puts his own stamp, or 'handwriting' on the vans in that range, and between them, the various makes provide the most comprehensive range of choices, sizes, styles and, of course, prices.

In addition to the above British manufacturers, there is a similar number of European manufacturers whose vans are distributed in the UK. These vary from the tiny Freedom models made in Poland to the solid German caravans with spacious accommodation and Teutonic build quality.

To study specific details of all the available models, and this includes size, weight, price, accommodation and many other factors, you can find all this information in the pages of the monthly caravan magazines. Practical Caravan publish every month a most comprehensive list of UK and European caravans, plus a detailed key to the 60 odd different internal layouts.

Don't think it ends there. On top of some twenty-eight brand names in current production, the pre-owned market offers several makes of good quality caravans which are no longer made, some having ceased production quite recently.

There is an enormous market in pre-owned caravans and for newcomers to the hobby they are a sensible and economic way of getting the feel of things. Caravan dealers always have a selection, and caravan magazines carry adverts for new and pre-owned vans.

To view the largest selection of all, however, let me point you to the internet and an enterprising initiative which can truly be described as providing a service to mankind. Go to caravanfinder. co.uk where, if you are after a particular make, size or price bracket, you will find the entire stock, both new and pre-owned from some 50 caravan dealers, plus over 1000 private sellers.

At the time of writing, Herself and I are in the process of buying a new caravan, and we sold our old one within a couple of weeks of advertising on the Caravan Finder website. The cost was £25 for 12 months exposure; the best £25 we have ever spent.

There is an enormous market in second hand caravans

The site has been operating for over 10 years and, in addition to caravans, has the largest selection of awnings in the UK.

If you are looking to sell your caravan, visit caravanfinder.co.uk, click on 'submit' and you're done and dusted within 5 minutes. The service is fast, efficient and hassle free. If you are a buyer, Caravan Finder has a truly gigantic choice, literally at your fingertips.

So having persuaded you that you have quite a wide selection to choose from, let's now talk about caravans.

The early American pioneer went west in a covered wagon, a horse-drawn, reasonably weatherproof bedroom-cum-living-room-cum-kitchen: in other words, a mobile home.

In the period between the two world wars, Romany families could be seen travelling around Britain and Europe in smaller but essentially similar wagons. The gypsy caravan was well known, gaily painted and comfortably fitted out with bed, cooking equipment and probably a small wood-burning stove.

My first experience of caravanning was as a very small boy in a similar outfit, except that it was towed behind my father's bull-nosed Morris. It was an Eccles caravan *(part of the Sterling range, they still make excellent caravans to this day)*. It had a bed, a table, a washbasin, a 'Primus' cooking stove, and it had delightful diamond-paned leaded windows, much like the photo on **page 4.**

That was well over 60 years ago, and during the following 20 years not much had changed. In the next 40 years, however, the touring caravan developed out of all recognition and in the process became subject to rules and regulations, all aimed at the welfare and safety of the caravanning and general public.

> You have quite a wide selection of caravans to choose from

■ *Bailey Senator Wyoming - 4 berth twin axle*

The earlier legislation was concerned mainly with road safety. Specifications were laid down for caravan chassis, car and caravan lighting, van brakes, maximum sizes, relative weights of van and car and, of course, speed limits, all designed to make the touring caravan safe on the roads.

Such legislation is constantly updated: both road and occupational safety measures are reviewed as ongoing items.

As technology marches relentlessly onwards, new standards are constantly being formulated to make caravans safe for the occupants. The use of both 12-volt and mains electricity; of propane and butane as fuels for cooking, heating and refrigeration; including air conditioning, standards of hygiene and fire safety; ventilation; the actual construction of the caravan - all these items and more are subjects of legislation designed to make caravanning safe, whether in transit or occupancy. Surprisingly, in the UK there is currently no regulatory approval process for checking that these many and varied standards are adhered to. This, in a nutshell, is what the National Caravan Council was set up to do. They have, for over 40 years, been checking that compliance with these standards is rigidly maintained.

To qualify for NCC badge of approval, each new or modified model is exhaustively checked, often being subject to over 600 separate inspections. Only then will the NCC's logo and Badge of Approval be granted. Foreign manufacturers will often modify their caravan or motorhome in order to qualify for the National Caravan Council's approval in the UK.

We will deal with the National Caravan Council in greater detail in a later chapter, but it is necessary, at this point, to make a potential caravanner aware of the NCC, to look for their approval logo on a caravan, and know what it stands for in terms of quality and safety.

With our increasing involvement with Europe, many of the British Standards relating to caravans have become merged with European Standards, new examples of which are constantly emerging. Where this will take us to, God knows - especially in the light of some partly apocryphal statistics with which I was regaled recently: ie the first verse of our National Anthem has 29 words, the Lord's Prayer has 69, the Ten Commandments contain 319 words, and the EU Directive on the Export of Duck eggs has 26,413.

There is a message in there somewhere.

So how have caravans changed? Well, 50 or 60 years ago caravans came in different sizes - as they do today - depending on how many they would sleep. Home comforts were few and far between, however. The kitchen area would have had either a paraffin-fuelled Primus stove or a gas ring fuelled by bottled Calor gas. There would

How have caravans changed?

have been a sink, complete with plug and waste pipe, but filling it with hot water involved boiling a kettle.

Lighting at night, once Calor gas had finally ousted the Primus stove, would have been by gaslights with incandescent mantles, and very homely and cosy they were.

The caravan might have had a toilet compartment, again with basin and waste pipe, but no tap. The loo was a portable affair with basically a bucket surmounted by a seat and a lid. In the absence of a toilet compartment, the loo went outside the van in a dedicated toilet tent.

Even with a toilet compartment in the caravan, many folk preferred to have the toilet outside in a small tent. Toilet tents are occasionally still seen in use today, in conjunction with older caravans.

We abandoned toilet tents years ago, following a brush with a sharp-horned cow in a Cornish field who took exception to our much travelled loo tent, and demolished it in the middle of the night. I still treasure the memory of Herself who, the following morning, driven by the urgencies of the moment, was to be seen perched upon the facilities, her head and shoulders sticking up through the remnants of our shredded loo tent, watched warily by the culprit cow from a few yards away. An idyllic rustic scene.

Then we started going soft and luxury became the order of the day. There's a saying in the motor trade to the effect that 'today's extras are tomorrow's standard fittings'. It's equally true of caravans, and over the next 40 years and up until today, each season saw quantum leaps forward in design, constructive safety, savings in weight and extra comfort and convenience.

Luxury has become the order of the day

■ **Above:** *Bailey Discovery Series 5 Neptune - 5 berth*

I do know that things become obvious with hindsight, but I must make the point that some of today's convenient features have been a long time coming.

We saw 12-volt electric lights, first powered from the towcar, then by a battery in the van. We had a tap at the kitchen sink and in the washroom. These were supplied by a footpump which retracted flush with the floor when not in use. Inevitably there followed 12-volt electric pumps, operated by the last word in micro-switches built into the actual tap. Hot water was next, actually heated and stored by a gas heater and tank concealed in a bed locker. Oh the joy of not having to boil a kettle in order to wash up.

When we first had a caravan which produced its own hot water supply, delivered by an electric pump to both kitchen sink and bathroom washbasin, I actually felt guilty. It smacked of sleeping in a tent and dining in a four-star restaurant a couple of hundred yards down the road.

Up to the mid-1950s, a caravan was little more than a shed on wheels, and in the 21st century we have come to the point where we virtually have a mobile home.

Hot running water, showers, flush toilets, television, CD players, central heating, air conditioning, rooms with fixed double beds, fridge/freezers, gas/electric hobs, ovens, microwaves, sunblinds, insect screens, where will it stop? They're not all like this, of course. These are the ultra modern, top-of-the-range, no-expense-spared jobs, and jogging along behind are literally thousands of not so new caravans, which have some of these features, are still very comfortable and give good service, so let's see what we've got.

At the end of the 1970s and the early 80s, radical changes in caravan construction took place.

For caravan walls, the old wooden framework gave way to a sandwich made of aluminium

Radical changes in construction took place in the 80's

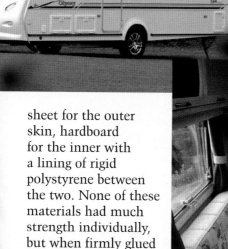

sheet for the outer skin, hardboard for the inner with a lining of rigid polystyrene between the two. None of these materials had much strength individually, but when firmly glued and bonded together the result was a

The NEW complete Caravan and Motor Home *Handbook*

composite material of considerable strength and rigidity plus good thermal insulation properties.

Floors were a similar bonded sandwich, the outer and inner skin being plywood. Even today, there are occasional instances of the floor sandwich coming unglued, at which point it loses its strength. This is known as 'delamination' and is a problem we will deal with later on.

Prior to this virtual revolution, caravans were built on a sturdy steel chassis, with heavy timber joists laid across them. The wooden floor was laid on top, as in house construction and on top of this came a lightweight timber framework, or skeleton. This had aluminium sheeting as outer cladding and usually a hardboard inner skin. Glass-fibre wool, as used in loft insulation would be sandwiched between the inner and outer skins, which would eventually slide down to floor level and become virtually useless.

At the same time bonded sandwich side walls, front and rear end walls and often roof would be made of

■ *Above: Bailey Paegeant - Series 6*

moulded fibreglass, stronger and lighter chassis were developed, suspension was improved, keeping pace with vehicle development. Away went the business of getting out of the car to engage the reverse catch when you wanted to drive the outfit backwards, the automatic reverse override took care of that.

Caravan windows took on a new form. Out went heavy glass, in came tinted acrylic material. Metal window frames were scrapped and double-glazing became possible at a lighter weight than the original single sheet of glass.

One of the quantum leaps was mains electricity. Virtually every new van is now equipped for mains voltage, opening up a whole world of in-van gadgetry - colour televisions, microwave ovens, kettles, toasters, space heaters, water heaters and so on.

The modern van gives you the choice of heating your water and indeed the caravan by either gas or mains electricity. We are

I now at the stage where much of the principle caravan lighting is via mains electricity, 12-volt being only used for illuminating cupboards, under shelves etc.

In the new millennium, caravan bodies weigh significantly less than their equivalent of 25 years ago. In most cases the weight saved has been used up by an ever-increasing wealth of sophisticated goodies which would have been unheard of in a 1960s caravan. You have a plumbed-in elegant toilet, washbasin and shower, plus spacious wardrobes, all in a closed off toilet and dressing area across the width of the rear end of your caravan. Large oven, even larger fridge, four-ring gas hob with automatic ignition, hot running water fuelled by either gas or main electricity are all featured and between them they are using up the weight saved by modern construction methods. You can have central heating or blown hot air, even air conditioning and the fridge may well have a deep-freeze compartment. The caravan is equipped with built-in television aerial, probably a radio/cassette and CD player as well. Tasteful furnishings, often to your own choice, window blinds in addition to curtains, a permanent in-situ double bed, plus micro-mesh insect screens to all windows and even the door - all are available with the modern caravan.

Technically it gets more complicated. You will have a 12/230 volt control and instrument panel which would do justice to the

Caravans
have steadily
become
more
sophisticated

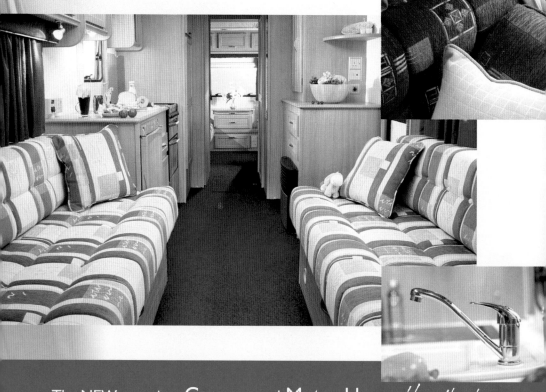

dashboard of a sports car. The mains circuit will incorporate a Residual Current Device which will trip out within milliseconds of any malfunction. There will be a facility for charging the caravan's 12-volt battery from the mains source. We seem to be approaching the point where the modern caravan cannot be improved on, but then I've been saying that for 25 years and yet caravans have steadily become more sophisticated.

This is a guide for all caravanners, regardless of how much they have to spend. Not all caravanners own this year's £20,000 supervan; many start by buying pre-owned, it's probably the best way to get the hang of things. You can acquire an old, basic, usable caravan for under £1000, or go the whole hog and spend over twenty-seven grand. Yes, that is the price of the top-of-the-range from Vanmaster, the Wigan-based company who currently build the Rolls Royce of caravans. Obviously the majority of caravans fall somewhere in between, and these are the ones we shall be talking about.

For lottery winners of course, there is always the American-sourced aluminium bodied heavyweight Airstream. This retails from around £38-£41,000 and is somewhat outside the scope of these humble jottings.

There are still caravans in use which are 25 years old or even more, many of them carrying famous names of caravan builders who, for one reason or another, are no longer in business. They are like vintage cars: the owners lavish much care and attention on their maintenance although they realise that the performance is not comparable with a current model. However, the caravan has begun to acquire both a rarity and sentimental value, and they would not part with it at any price.

1970 was a significant date in build terms

It is for this reason that I make no apology for the occasional reference to vans with, for example, gas lighting, or a single cold water tap at the sink. However, caravans of 1970 vintage or earlier are unlikely to change hands very frequently nowadays. I pick 1970 deliberately because it was a significant date in terms of build quality to a laid down standard.

Any British caravan built from 1970 onwards had to conform to British Standard no. 4626, which was designed to cover caravan safety from various points of view eg chassis, brakes, 12-volt electric wiring, use of gas *(LPG)* etc.

The provisions of BS 4626 were superseded some 20 years later by a revised standard, BS 6765. This was an updating process made necessary by the onward march of technology, for example, the installation of mains *(220/230)* voltage electricity in caravans.

At about this time the spectre of the all-enveloping European Community was taking shape, and parts of the recently formed BS 6765 were put on hold pending the formulation, with international cooperation, of a set of new European standards.

On the basis that the amount of business achieved by a committee is in inverse proportion to the number of members present, these standards took some considerable time to take shape.

The effect of this legislation is to guard the health and safety of today's caravanners with the same sort of strict manufacturing precautions as you would find in the production of, say, pork pies or proprietary medicines.

I doubt if one per cent of potential caravanners will trouble to note the details in the following paragraph, but the book would be incomplete without them. So, current British/EU standards are now as follows:

BNEN 1645,	*part 1*,	covers health and safety in areas of habitation
BNEN 1645,	*part 2*,	covers payload (weight carried)
BNEN 1648,	*part 1*,	covers 12 volt electrics
BNEN 721,		covers ventilation
BNEN 60335,		safety of electrical appliances
EN 1949,		covers LPG (liquefied petroleum gas)
BS 6765,	*part 4*,	covers chassis and undergear

These standards have virtually replaced the former BS 4626, and all European *(which includes British)* caravans built to 1999 and onwards' specifications will conform to these rigid standards, which have been formulated to ensure maximum levels of road and occupational safety.

Provided that it is regularly and properly serviced and maintained a caravan will give good service for many years. Neglect your caravan in this area and you will be putting yourself and your family at risk, both in occupation and on the road. More on service and maintenance later.

We'll look at caravans in more detail shortly, but before starting to choose the van, you must consider what you're going to tow it with.

The Towcar to match the Caravan

What your car can comfortably tow is most important. There is an old adage that says you should have the smallest caravan you can comfortably live in, towed by the largest car you can afford. Although this is a bit extreme it is good advice and you should try not to allow the Actual Laden Weight *(ALW)* of your van to exceed 85% of the kerbside weight of your car. *(The ALW is the ex-works weight of your van plus all its contents. We will see in a later chapter how the contents rapidly add up to a formidable amount of weight.)* Manufacturers will state a Maximum Laden Weight (MLW) for a van. This is the very maximum weight for which the caravan is designed for normal use when being towed on the road laden. The ALW should always be kept below the MLW. You could be outside the law if the MLW is exceeded. Although there is no specific regulation to this effect, the law might decide that 'the weight, distribution, packing and adjustment of the load' caused or might cause danger on a road. *(Construction and Use Regulation 100.)*

Tow only what is comfortable for your car

The kerbside weight of your car is its weight delivered new, ie with fuel, oil and water plus wheelbrace and jack, but with no non-standard equipment or luggage. Keeping the actual laden weight of your caravan down to 85% of the kerb weight of your car is a piece of advice which you will see referred to many times in caravan magazines. I would stress, however, that it is advice aimed at the new caravanner - one without towing experience. When some of this experience has been gained, the weight of the caravan can be allowed to get nearer to the kerbweight of the car. If you know what you are about, you can almost equate caravan/car weights on a 1 to 1 basis.

You should be accurate here, since if you allow any trailer to exceed 100% of the car's kerbside weight, you could be outside the law under the Construction and Use regulations. We shall see that a similar offence occurs if the laden weight of the van exceeds the stated Maximum Laden Weight.

These expressions are fairly easy to understand. The Maximum Laden Weight, set by the caravan manufacturer, is the absolute limit of weight that the chassis and suspension can safely carry. The Actual Laden Weight is the total weight of the van after you have put all your gear in it, and of course this should never exceed the MLW, better that it should be less than the MLW by a safe margin. The 'payload' of the caravan is the difference between the ex-works weight, ie a totally empty caravan, and the Maximum Laden Weight.

Now here I must try to avoid confusing you, but 1999 and later caravans have their various weights referred to by a new set of terminology, prompted by the adoption of EN 1645 part 2.

The phrases Maximum Laden Weight and Actual Laden Weight are easy to understand and I include them here because they will feature in the owners' handbooks of countless pre-1999 caravans.

Now, however, European standards require us to use new expressions of weight. Maximum Technical Permissible Laden Mass *(MTPLM)* is Eurospeak for Maximum Laden Weight. Yes, really!

What used to be the ex-works weight is now termed the Mass in Running Order *(MRO)*, and the User Payload - formerly the Caravan Allowable Payload - is the weight of all the equipment and supplies you load into the van. This includes caravan battery, gas cylinders and all your personal clothing, pots and pans, crockery, TV set, etc. If you wish to splash out on an air conditioner, the weight of this must be included in your user payload, as must any electric caravan mover equipment which is permanently attached to the caravan.

If you subtract the MRO from the MTPLM - go on, think about it - you will arrive at the weight of your load, or User Payload. Your loaded caravan should, ideally, weigh a little less than the manufacturer's stated Maximum Technical Permissible Laden Mass.

> Never exceed your Maximum Laden Weight

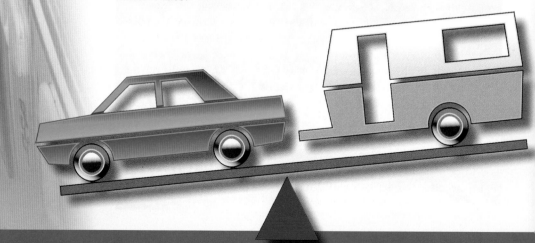

MTPLM, MRO *(Mass in Running Order)* and User Payload are the three commonly used terms in caravan publications to describe the vital weight statistics of any modern van.

Whatever terms you use, remember never to allow your loaded caravan to weigh more than your towcar's kerbside weight.

Consider, finally, one further expression, ie Maximum Train Weight. This is the combined weight of both loaded car and loaded caravan. It will be stipulated in the car's handbook, and must never be exceeded.

Do note that if you tow your caravan when it exceeds the stated Maximum Technical Permissible Laden mass, you could be outside the law, and putting your safety and that of other road users in jeopardy.

We have rather strayed away from the subject of the towcar, but before we talked about the relative weights of car and caravan, it was important to be clear about which caravan weight we are referring to. Let's now get back to the car.

Weight and engine size of car

This van/car weight ratio is vital in arriving at a safe and manageable road outfit, but in addition to the weight of the car you must also consider its engine size and its resultant power and torque. Many 'high performance' cars, particularly those with comparatively small engines, ie around 1600/1800 cc, tend to develop their peak performance at fairly high engine speeds.

Diesel-engined cars are good for towing

It is little use trying to tow with a car whose towing muscle is achieved at about 3200 rpm or so. The maximum permitted towing speed in the UK is 60 mph, and only then on dual carriageways.

It is for this reason that diesel-engined cars are so good for towing. Year after year we find the prestigious 'Towcar of the year' award is won by a diesel-powered car. Diesel engines develop peak torque, or pulling power, at much lower engine speeds. They therefore tow comfortably and economically at around 50-mph. Driven solo, a diesel will always prove more economical than a petrol-engined vehicle. Adding a caravan to the load will lower the mpg figures less dramatically with a diesel power unit.

Towing really calls for a willing workhorse rather than a spirited thoroughbred.

It is not enough to be able to tow your caravan on a level road. You may have to start the outfit off from standstill on a gradient, preferably without burning out your clutch. How much power is needed?

A good rule of thumb is to have a car whose engine can produce a minimum of 40-brake horsepower *(BHP)* per ton of outfit weight. That is total weight of car and caravan combined. This sounds a bit complicated but it is simple to calculate.

Take an average family saloon car with turbo-diesel engine producing 110 BHP. Its kerb *(unladen)* weight would be about 1410 kg.

Now add an equally average 4 berth caravan with a body length of, say, 4.0 metres, and this would have a MTPLM of about 1150 kg.

Now we have a car *(A)*, kerb weight 1410 kg towing a caravan, *(B)* with a max. laden weight of 1150 kg. In this case, B is 81.6% of A. Fine, so the van is comfortably inside the recommended 85% of the kerb weight of the car, which we referred to a couple of pages back.

Now, is the car powerful enough to pull the van?

We said we wanted at least 40 Brake Horse Power *(BHP)* per ton of the weight of the whole outfit. So what does the whole outfit weigh?

Well, the maximum weight of the loaded caravan *(MTPLM)* is 1150 kg. The kerb *(unladen weight)* of the car is 1410 kg, but we must add to this the usual stuff you load in a car, plus the weight of, in this case, two passengers plus their luggage, say 180 kg.

The total outfit weight is therefore 1150 + 1410 + 180 = 2740 kg. Now if you will accept the fact that one ton is near enough 1015 kg, and we divide our 2740 Kgs by 1015, we come up with 2.7 tons as the total weight of car, caravan, people and luggage.

Ideally we wanted 40 BHP per ton of outfit weight, so in this case we have 2.7 tons x 40 BHP = 108. Our turbodiesel car produces 110 BHP, which is enough 'grunt' for the task, so it would seem to be an acceptable tow car for the caravan in terms of both weight and power.

Two points are worth making here *(1)* the MTPLM of the caravan is the prescribed maximum, but if you have not used up all of your User Payload, the actual weight of the van could be less

The NEW complete Caravan and Motor Home *Handbook*

than the stated 1150 kg, so giving you a greater safety margin, and *(2)* this 85% weight ratio between loaded caravan and kerb weight of car is not a rigid rule, nor is it law -- it's a useful guide. It's aimed at the novice caravanner, as stated earlier, and once more experience in towing is gained you can perhaps afford to increase the weight behind the car. Make no mistake though, if the weight of the loaded caravan ever EXCEEDS the kerb weight of the towcar, it is illegal and actually dangerous.

The rule of thumb has served well enough for some considerable time, but as cars become more sophisticated, so does the arithmetic. Many car manufacturers express the power of their engines in terms other than brake horsepower

Engine output *(torque)* can be expressed in ft/lbs or kilowatts or NM *(Newton metres)*.

Now this is getting a bit over the top. This is not a textbook but a simple guide to a straightforward subject, so I am not going to blind you with conversion tables which correlate all these various units of power. Our simple formula of 40 brake horse power per ton of outfit weight *(ie car plus caravan)* is a good rough guide, but do remember the question of pulling power, in other words 'torque'. An engine which produces peak torque at low revs is best for towing, and that usually means diesel. If your car handbook doesn't deal in brake horsepower, go to a qualified car dealer and ask him to convert it for you.

Good tow cars have a fairly close-ratio gearbox

A good towcar will ideally have a fairly close-ratio gearbox, ie not too wide a gap between gears, particularly between fourth and fifth.

Engine power and gear ratios could take up a chapter by themselves, but this is not intended as a technical thesis. It is sufficient to say that the most economical solo cars are by no means the most economical towcars. You must have sufficient power from your engine to have a little in reserve when towing.

To arrive quickly at the likely laden weight of the caravan, subtract the Mass in Running Order from the Maximum Technical Permissible Running Mass *(see the caravan handbook)*. This figure gives the van's User Payload. Since this is the absolute maximum permissible, you should aim at a little less than the 'book' payload as the amount of gear you will load in the caravan.

How on earth do I calculate that? Well, it's not easy, but the simple answer is to take your loaded caravan to a public weighbridge, and make sure it does not exceed the manufacturer's Maximum Technical Permissible Laden Mass.

In the past some caravans were advertised as having artificially low MTPLMs. This appeared to make them towable by fairly small cars, but this was only achieved by leaving a very small allowance for loading luggage and accessories, ie 'payload'. BS 4626 put a stop to this and defined the payload allowance as follows: it must be a minimum of 15% of MTPLM plus an allowance of 15 kg for gas cylinders, plus another 15 kg if no heater is fitted, plus another 30 kg if there is no refrigerator.

Since some of your weights are metric and some imperial, the following guide might be helpful for your calculations:

> **10 kg equals 22 lb.**
> **10 lb equals 4.54 kg.**

Towsafe linked up with HPI a couple of years ago

All this talk of caravan/car weights sounds off-putting but it is simple in principle and quite vital to the stability, safety and sometimes the legality of your outfit. You must never exceed the recommended MTPLM of your caravan, and never allow it to exceed the kerb weight of your car. Ideally, the caravan/car-towing ratio should be 85% for inexperienced caravanners.

We have now taken you through the principal calculations of matching car to caravan, and vice versa. You now know why you shouldn't attempt to tow an 18 foot twin axle van with a Nissan Micra, so let me now point you towards someone who can do all these sums for you, someone who can match your car and caravan impartially, accurately and infallibly.

Towsafe linked up with HPI some years ago. HPI are the company who offer a comprehensive check on vehicles - former 'write-offs', checks on mileages, outstanding finance, etc. They also operate the Caravan Registration and Identity Scheme *(CRiS)*, which we will look at in detail in the chapter on Security.

Towsafe can give you a match between any combination of caravan and car, advising you on suitability or otherwise.

By phoning **HPI/Towsafe** on **01722 411430** you can obtain a report on the suitability of a specific car to a specific caravan for a fee of £9.95, or by visiting www.towsafe.co.uk online, you can receive advice on five different combinations for £15.95.

Additionally, and by telephone only, you can get a list of 100 caravans which match a particular car, or 100 cars to match a particular van. From this list you can then receive a report on a one-to-one combination for £7.95.

The Towsafe service is also available at most UK main caravan dealers, where a charge may or may not be made.

If you are at all unsure about safely matching a car and caravan, this is a small price to pay for peace of mind.

Useful Number:
HPI/Towsafe: 01722 411430

Matching caravan to car

1   What is the Maximum Laden Weight or MTPLM of your proposed caravan? ✓

2   What is its weight ex-works (ie empty) or the MRO? Remember that the figure given by the manufacturer may vary by + or - 5% in practice. Check the actual figure on a weighbridge. ✓

3   Subtract 2 from 1 to calculate the payload available. Is this adequate? (See Page 129 for weights of essential extra equipment). ✓

4   What is the kerbside weight of your car? Is the laden weight of the van less than this, preferably no more than 85% for new players? ✓

5   Does your car engine produce at least 40 BHP for every ton of 'outfit weight'? (This is the combined weight of loaded caravan and loaded car.) ✓

6   If you cannot answer 'yes' to 3, 4 and 5 you are looking at the wrong caravan, or need a larger car. It is important to be careful with public weighbridges. Their accuracy is questionable with relatively light loads such as a caravan. ✓

Choosing a Caravan and a suitable tow car

■ **Above:** *Side dinette converts to two bunk beds.*

■ **Right:** *Bailey Senator with fixed bed.*

Accommodation and Size of Caravan

Having decided on the weight of a caravan your car can tow, you can now narrow things down a little by considering how many people it must sleep.

Consider how many people you want to sleep

Two-berth caravans can vary from the 10 foot ultra-cramped models to the obscenely spacious and luxurious. The last word in this latter class arrived with the millennium. Caravans with a room containing a fixed double bed, no less, in some cases en suite with the washroom, rapidly caught on and most manufacturers now include such a model in their range.

It can be classed as a four berth, with two single berths or a double in the front lounge area, and then the fixed double aft. It can, of course, be used as a two berth, leaving the front lounge area solely as a sitting room. The final option is for occasions when you're not speaking to each other and then you can sleep at opposite ends of the caravan.

Opinions seem to be divided between a fixed double bed being a staggeringly brilliant idea or an appalling waste of space. The only virtue, as I see it, is to save the fiddly business of making up beds in the lounge area at night, otherwise I'm with the waste of space school. Time will tell, and I'm probably wrong.

Four- to five-berth vans are commonplace and may be in the 12 foot to 15 foot body length group. Six-berth vans tend to be from 14 foot to 16 foot or even up to 20 feet, although there are many ingenious designs which incorporate children's or larger beds which fold away out of sight in the daytime, producing surprisingly generous sleeping facilities at night in quite modestly sized caravans. *(These arrangements, however, can often be at the expense of sufficient space to operate freely in the kitchen area, or they may hinder opening the toilet door fully.)* It is important also to check that, when children are in bed, there is absolutely unrestricted access to the caravan exit door at all times, in the even of fire.

Sleeping, cooking and dining

Caravans with more than two berths usually provide a double bed in the front sitting/dining area, plus perhaps another double bed at the rear of the caravan or a number of single bunks, often one above the other. These multi-berth layouts usually place the kitchen area on one side of the caravan - amidships - whereas a two-berth caravan has a double bonus. The arrangement is usually one bed of at least 6 feet x 6 feet 6 inches or two roomy singles, and the kitchen is along the rear wall of the caravan. This is known as an 'end kitchen' and is roomier than the sidewall variety. It is made possible by the absence of beds, bunks, etc at the rear end. The cupboards and toilet compartment are also correspondingly roomier in a two-berth caravan.

Alternatively, a roomy two-berth can feature the large double bed at the front end, have the kitchen along a side wall, leaving scope for a spacious shower/toilet/dressing room, complete with wardrobe, across the entire width of the caravan at the rear end.

Roomy two-berth caravans can feature a large double bed

■ **Right:** *Bailey Ranger washroom*

Awning

Finally, on the subject of how many beds you want, think about an awning. An awning is a weatherproof type of tent, joined simply and firmly to the side of the van. It has a framework of lightweight poles, and can effectively more than double the living space of your caravan. A brood of children, therefore, need not bar you from caravanning, or commit you to an over-large caravan. When our four children were small, we slept at least two of them on comfortable inflatable beds in the awning and also used it for storing folding chairs and table, tinned food, beach mats, wellies and all the other junk a family collects on holiday.

More about awnings in *Chapter 5.*

An awning can more than double your living space

Checklist:

Accommodation

1 Two-person families need a two-berth caravan, which is no problem, or a 4 berth as a luxury. ✓

2 For larger families, could you sleep the children in a caravan awning, or even in a separate tent? Given this solution, does the caravan enable you all to eat together? ✓

3 Is the layout convenient for your needs? ✓

4 Are the beds adequate for extra tall or wide crew members? ✓

5 Is there sufficient wardrobe/locker space for all the clobber for larger crews? ✓

6 Could you be 'at home' in the caravan? Does it feel right? ✓

Trailer Tents and Folding Campers

If the crossword clue is 'a mobile unit of habitation towed behind a vehicle', the answer is not necessarily 'caravan'.

Having described caravans in some detail, this might be an appropriate point at which to mention a lightweight alternative, albeit only briefly.

Trailer tents and folding campers have certain advantages over caravans, but without all the sophisticated comforts. You are unlikely to find a cocktail cabinet in a trailer tent. Having said this, the specifications can include a fridge, mains voltage electrics, a toilet compartment, a fitted kitchen and sundry other goodies.

The basic unit folds down into a compact trailer, typically some 8 feet long by 6 feet wide by 4 feet high. Towing is therefore simpler than with a caravan, there being full vision through the car's rear-view mirror and virtually no aerodynamic drag.

Family living space can be surprisingly generous

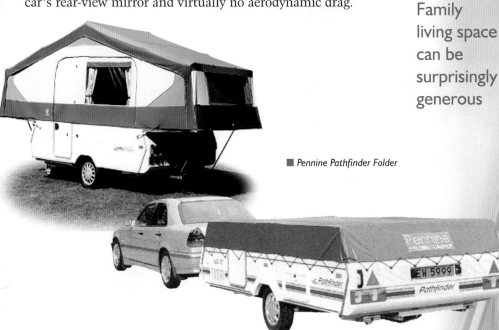

■ *Pennine Pathfinder Folder*

The photographs show a camper folded for towing, and opened out ready for occupation. If an awning or dedicated frame tent is added, the amount of living space available for a family can be surprisingly generous.

This is probably an important feature because, over the years, I have noticed that caravanners and campers seem to reproduce at a fairly prolific rate. Summer campsites seem often to echo to the various cries of kids in the process of being beaten to a pulp by siblings.

Our brood was no exception. Our first caravan was a £320 second-hand 10 foot Lynton, into which Herself and I managed to shoehorn ourselves and four children. It was a bit cramped.

All this recalls a vividly remembered piece of advice by an elderly gent who was proposing the health of the happy couple at their wedding. With hindsight, he said, he had come to the conclusion that the best time to have children was in one's mid-seventies, since you were going to be up and about three or four times a night anyway.

But I'm wandering again. This book is about caravanning and I don't intend to go banging on about trailer tents and folding campers. I mention them because they are an alternative, with pluses and minuses like anything else.

One significant advantage of folders is that of on-the-road weight, which can be around 50% of the weight of a caravan. A much lower profile makes for better fuel economy when towing and gives better rear vision. All this, of course, opens up a much wider choice of possible towcars.

Internal features

In addition to innovations in basic construction, internal equipment has made great steps forward. Since the mid to late 1980s caravans have been equipped with hot water systems, electrically pumped water supply, toilet compartments with showers and built-in flushing toilets. Warmth is provided by thermostatically controlled hot air or hot water central heating systems. Built in hi-fi systems are often now included, and since about 1990, mains electricity has been virtually standard.

Older caravans without heating or mains electricity can often be adapted to include either or both.

Additions and modifications

Caravans which are sound in wind and limb, but 20 years old or more, are still to be found at bargain prices but may well be without heating, electric water pump, hot water system, fridge or oven. All these can be supplied and installed by a competent DIY man or a caravan dealer's workshop. If you are going to install gas appliances yourself, however, do have your finished system pressure-checked at a dealer's workshop, to ensure that it is absolutely free of leaks.

Mains electricity in caravans is not quite so straightforward as in household use. Safety factors are of paramount importance, and installing mains on a DIY basis is to be discouraged. Get it done professionally. **See *Chapter 6 - mains electrics.***

Installing mains on a DIY basis is to be discouraged

Remember that all these extras constitute additional weight. Watch your recommended MTPLM. In this connection, two heavy items are the fridge and the oven. If you wish to install either of these and you can afford only one because of either cost or weight, go for the fridge every time. Even an average English summer will see your milk, meat, butter, etc. 'going off' in no time, and for continental summer holidays a fridge is a must.

You can go on adding extras indefinitely. For example, I installed a car radio/cassette player and two speakers in our previous van. I also added a CD player, a standard feature in many modern vans

To sum up then, the less you pay for your van the greater will be its probable age and weight, and the fewer modern amenities it will have. If you have a fixed amount to spend, bear in mind that to remain within your budget **it may be better to buy a good quality, well-appointed caravan that is three or four years old and has been well maintained, than to buy a brand new caravan from the lower end of the price range, with a more basic specification.**

With a family, it is also more sensible to buy a medium-size van and a good awning, than a large van to sleep everybody. The larger caravan will be more expensive, heavier and less manageable, and will need a larger car to tow it.

The new versus second-hand decision is, at the end of the day, up to you. Of course brand new is nicer: it's like a new car, it has a lovely 'new' smell to it, and nobody has had their hands on it but you.

The first touring caravan went on sale around 100 years ago

It is a fact that since the first touring caravan went on sale around 100 years ago, each year has seen new models that were in some way an advance on the previous year.

The process continues, particularly in the troublesome area of damp and leaks or water ingress, as the manufacturers like to call it.

For the 2004 range, Bailey instituted a six-year warranty against water ingress damage **AND** panel delamination. These are in addition to Bailey's normal three-year warranty on component defects, and other makers are following.

So the newer your caravan, the more technically advanced it will be, which is not to say that there are not many sound, comfortable vans available which are several years old and therefore considerably cheaper than a new one.

Unless money is no object, then new versus pre-owned is something you need to consider very carefully. If you do go for pre-owned, however, then do buy from a reputable source.

Pre-owned caravans

Before selling a pre-owned caravan a dealer must thoroughly check it on all points where safety is involved. If it proves faulty the dealer is liable. No such redress is available with a private sale.

A pre-owned caravan, like a pre-owned car, can hide a basketful of unsuspected faults. The National Caravan Council put out a leaflet detailing all the reasons why it makes sense to buy a pre-owned van from a reputable dealer, one who is a member of the NCC.

You will pay a bit more for a pre-owned van from a dealer than if you had bought it from the previous owner, **BUT** it will have been thoroughly inspected, including the all-important checks on damp, gas, 12 and 230 volt electrics, chassis, suspension and brakes, to name only a few, and any faults rectified. It will have been properly serviced and it will probably come to you with some form of guarantee.

Of course many caravans do change hands privately every year, and with no regrets, and if you want to do this, I would only advise you to take another caravanner with you who really knows what he is about. The following are just some of the points you should be looking at.

Before the advent of polystyrene sandwich construction, caravans were built on a timber framework, and some of them are still in use. Even modern caravans using sandwich construction employ some wood framework within the sandwich. Moisture can eat into this framework, so it is essential to check carefully corners and seams in the metal outer cladding of the caravan and around window frames. Look for dried-out, flaking mastic filler.

Check for damp stains throughout the interior. Carefully and thoroughly inspect the entire chassis and corner steadies for rust. The same applies to brake linkages. Does the handbrake hold the caravan on a slope?

Check for damp stains around water and waste-pipe joints. Check front and rear light clusters for damp. Gas leaks are dangerous, but easily checked on. Check the tyres, less for tread wear than splits in the grooves, and tyre walls for cuts, splits or bulges. Are they a matching pair for type and size? Walk the length of the floor inside the caravan. If any part of it feels soft or spongy, the floor is probably in the process of delaminating, which we mentioned earlier.

Many caravans change hands privately every year

A modern caravan floor is a layer of styrene sandwiched between two sheets of plywood, all three being glued together under pressure. If the glue fails, the sandwich starts to come apart and the strength of the floor is lost. This is delamination and calls for a repair job in a dealer's workshop. The area concerned can be re-glued in situ, but if you suspect a floor in a second-hand van is delaminating - give it a miss.

Carefully check the upholstery and carpet for signs of excess wear, dirt or *(perish the thought)* cigarette burns. There are a dozen ways in which to form an impression of how the previous owners have treated what is possibly going to be **YOUR** caravan. If they come across as being finicky and houseproud to the point of being a pain in the neck, then you've probably got a good buy.

An important item to check, whether buying privately or from a dealer, is when the caravan in question last had a damp check. Ask to see the written report which always accompanies a damp check during an annual service.

Ask to see invoices from previous periodic services; be suspicious if none is available. Check the chassis number on older vans - this is usually found on a metal plate fixed to the drawbar or die-stamped on to the frame. Plates with false numbers are too easily switched. A phone call to the chassis manufacturer or caravan dealer will confirm the age of the van. In case of difficulty in tracing the manufacturer, contact the Caravan Club or the National Caravan Council.

See *Useful Contacts* at the back of the book.

If the caravan is post-1991 it will be registered under the Caravan Registration and Identification Scheme *(CRiS)* and it will have its CRiS registration number etched onto all windows. Ask to see the registration document, and you could also ring the CRiS section at HPI to check the CRiS scheme for the **National Caravan Council**. They can be contacted on **01722 411430**.

See the section on CRiS in *Chapter 11 - on security.*

There is now a rapidly growing availability of second-hand caravans on the internet. Try **RVsales.co.uk** or **www. caravanfinder.co.uk**

If you are buying privately, go to the home of the vendor, and make sure that that is where he really lives, and that he is the bona fide present owner of the van. Don't let the vendor bring the van to you - he could be flogging a dodgy or 'hot' caravan, and wishing to remain anonymous.

Check chasis numbers on older vans

Take the caravan for a trial tow, if possible, before you decide to buy. Does it sit level viewed from the end? Does it handle well and feel right? Don't feel hesitant about asking the history of a caravan you propose to buy. If you are offered a pre-owned van at a suspiciously low price or you have doubts about its origin, note the chassis number and model, then make a phone call to either the Caravan Club or the National Caravan Council. Both keep a computerised record of all stolen caravans.

If you have the misfortune to buy a caravan which subsequently proves to be stolen then you are the loser. It legally belongs to the person from whom it was stolen, and your purchase money goes down the drain. Your only redress is from the one who stole it, and assuming you can find him, sueing him is unlikely to bear fruit. Alternatively, if the dealer or person you bought it from is proved to have knowingly received stolen goods then you have a claim against him, but it is a costly, tedious and unpleasant business, so do be warned. There are stolen caravans about, and many are offered for resale.

Always consider the extras you might need before buying

Unscrupulous caravan dealers are, happily, few and far between, but not totally non-existent. In his eagerness to make a sale, don't let some wise guy persuade you that, say, a two berth Swift Silhouette which has taken your fancy would be an ideal match for your 1100cc Ford Escort. Do heed the detailed advice given earlier in this chapter about engine power, plus kerb weight of car and laden weight of caravan. Don't let your enthusiasm run away with you over an attractive-looking pre-owned caravan (or car). You **MUST** match the car to the caravan and the caravan to the car, or you could be wasting hard earned money.

Finally, before spending your last cent on a caravan, consider the extras it may need. If your caravan is pre-owned some of these items may be included, and the dealer could well supply some items pre-owned. You will certainly need two gas cylinders, plus a regulator valve and fresh and wastewater containers. A fire extinguisher plus a fire blanket are strongly recommended, as is a 12-volt battery. A water trolley makes life easier (a five-gallon container of water weights 50 lb!). A spare wheel plus jack and wheelbrace are essentials, and finally, perhaps on lower priority, come a fridge, if not fitted, and suitable awning.

See Chapter 5 - awnings.

caravan construction

1 The older the caravan you are considering, the heavier it is likely to be (and the more likely to leak).

2 Check seams and corners of body for damp. Check chassis and drawbar for anything more than superficial rust, and for structural weakness.

3 Check corner steadies (the wind-down legs).

4 Check brakes (including handbrake) and tyres.

5 Check for water and gas leaks.

6 Check electrics.

7 Check that you don't have a 'spongey' floor inside the caravan.

8 Check manufacturer's name and chassis number.

9 Unless you are buying an old, low-priced caravan, buy from a reputable dealer.

10 If you are not confident that you know what you're about - take along someone who does. It could save you a lot of regret.

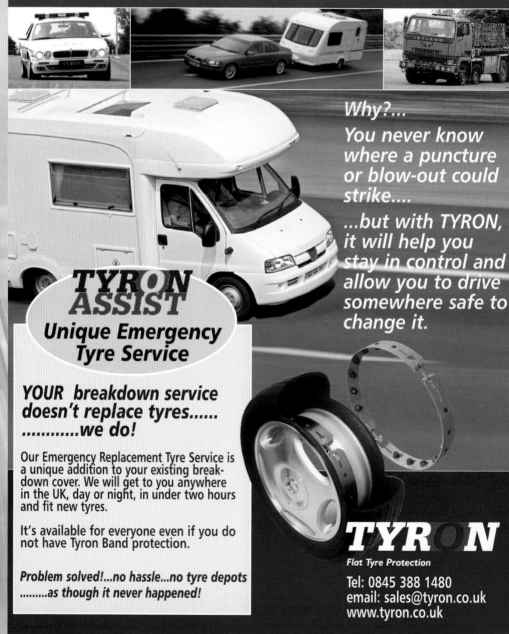

Police Forces and the Military use Tyron Flat Tyre Protection - So should you!

TYRON ASSIST
Unique Emergency Tyre Service

YOUR breakdown service doesn't replace tyres...... ....we do!

Our Emergency Replacement Tyre Service is a unique addition to your existing break-down cover. We will get to you anywhere in the UK, day or night, in under two hours and fit new tyres.

It's available for everyone even if you do not have Tyron Band protection.

Problem solved!...no hassle...no tyre depots ....as though it never happened!

Why?...
You never know where a puncture or blow-out could strike....

...but with TYRON, it will help you stay in control and allow you to drive somewhere safe to change it.

TYRON
Flat Tyre Protection

Tel: 0845 388 1480
email: sales@tyron.co.uk
www.tyron.co.uk

Towing
on the Road

Towbars or Towing brackets

Before getting down to details on towing let us deal with the obvious fact that your car cannot tow anything, even a little 5 cwt garden trailer, unless it is fitted with a towbar.

When you have a towbar fitted to your car you will also have towing 'electrics' fitted. This means fitting two suitably wired sockets to the rear of the vehicle so that 12-volt current can be supplied to the caravan to cater for quite a wide variety of needs. These include road lights for the outside of the caravan plus various internal supply points for 12-volt accessories. These are dealt with in more detail in **Chapter 5 - 12-volt electricity**. At this point we are dealing with the actual towbar itself, not the wiring.

Towbars vary widely in detail and price. Many upmarket cars need to be fitted with the car manufacturer's own towbar to avoid nullifying the warranty, and these can be expensive. However this is less likely if a type approved towbar is fitted to a post-August 1998 car *(see next page)*.

There are specialist towbar manufacturers who produce towbars to fit almost any model of car. Most cars are supplied with dedicated towbar fixing points and it will be a condition of the vehicle warranty that any towbar fitted to the car must use ALL the fixing points provided. Failure to comply with this requirement would invalidate the car's warranty and also cause the failure of any insurance claim in the event of a towing related incident.

As we said earlier, some car manufacturers will only allow the fitting of their own towbars, but they are in the minority. These 'own make' towbars, apart from being expensive, are not always a good bet. They often take the form of a 'swan neck' fitting, which has no attachment point for the two 12-volt electric sockets which are needed, nor is there provision for the attachment of a breakaway or safety chain, of which more later.

**Towbars
vary widely
in detail
and price**

2

Towbars consist of an assembly of metal bars *(sometimes angle iron)* which, when fitted, present a flat vertical surface to the rear, usually just below the rear bumper. This surface has two holes drilled into it, a few inches apart, and to these holes is bolted the towball unit.

The towball is a short, sturdy, curved piece of steel which is surmounted by a standard 50mm 'ball', and it is to this ball that the tow hitch or coupling head of the caravan is fixed when van and car are 'hitched' together.

Towbars are supplied by a variety of manufacturers and there has not always been a guarantee of quality. Not any more - the long arm of Brussels has reached out, yea brethren, even unto towbars.

Any car first registered on or after 1st August 1998 *(S reg)*, if used for towing, must be fitted with an EC Type Approved towbar. Type approval is only granted after rigorous testing. A Type Approved towbar will carry a label, plate or stamp certifying that it conforms to the relevant 'E' number ie 94/20/EC.

All this applies only to post-August 1st 1998 cars, ie 'S' registered.

Legislation now makes a breakaway cable mandatory

Note that the Ford 'Ka', that little curvy number that you either love or loathe, was not declared by Ford as suitable for towing, so there is no Type Approved towbar. Towing with it, or even fitting some kind of towbar could render one liable to prosecution, in addition to nullifying the vehicle warranty. The same applies to the MG 'F' sports car. It is not designed for towing.

The supervision and enforcement of these new regulations *(Directive 94/20 EC)* rests with local Trading Standards officers. The requirement is the subject of an amendment to the current Construction and Use Regulations, and failure to comply is not only a traffic offence, but it may well invalidate the car's insurance. If you fit a towbar to a second-hand car, therefore, do check its date of first registration.

We mentioned earlier a safety or breakaway cable. European legislation now makes a breakaway cable mandatory. It is a simple steel cable attached to the lower end of the caravan's handbrake, and the other end is fastened, via a quick release clasp, to an eye on the car's towbar.

The purpose of this device is to cater for the very unlikely event of the caravan coupling head becoming detached from the towball, or failure of the actual towball itself. In either of these events, the caravan becomes separated from the tow car, but before the breakaway cable itself actually fails, it automatically applies the caravan brakes as the gap between van and car increases.

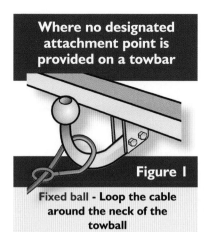

Where no designated attachment point is provided on a towbar

Figure 1

Fixed ball - Loop the cable around the neck of the towball

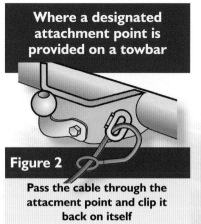

Where a designated attachment point is provided on a towbar

Figure 2

Pass the cable through the attacment point and clip it back on itself

Some vehicle manufacturers' own make of towbar often fall short here, in that they do not provide a fixing point for a breakaway cable. This applies particularly to detachable and 'swan neck' towballs as shown in figure 1. **See the section on hitching up later in this chapter.**

In May 2003 the National Caravan Council issued a guidance leaflet on the recommended manner of fixing a breakaway cable to the towbar. The preferred method is as shown in figure 2, where, in the event of the trailer becoming detached from the towball, the application of the handbrake would not depend on the strength of the clip, which would be the case with the fastening as shown in figure 1.

It should be noted that, once attached, the breakaway cable should have enough slack to prevent the cable applying the handbrake when the outfit is being driven round corners. This has been recorded as being the major cause of a number of unpleasant towing accidents. Too much slack, on the other hand, can cause the cable to drag on the ground, ultimately weakening it to the point of failure.

Note that the law makes the use of a breakaway cable mandatory on all braked trailers which, of course, includes all caravans.

Always rely on the side mirrors

Towing mirrors

New legislation on towing mirrors applies from January 26th 2010. On cars registered AFTER this date, towing mirrors may project up to 25cms. outside the car. Prior to this date 20cm. was the maximum projection. For some time now the offside towing mirror had to be adjustable from the driver's seat. Thanks to National Caravan Council for this information.

On the road

The caravan will faithfully follow the path of the towing vehicle, except for a tendency for the van to slightly cut corners. If, for example, you turn left into a side road, and you steer the car close to the kerb in the process, the caravan's nearside wheel could mount the kerb.

This tendency to cut corners depends to some extent on how much 'overhang' there is between the car's back wheels and the towball. The distance from the axle back to the towball on a smallish hatchback is considerably less than the same measurement on, say, a Volvo Estate. The closer the towball is to the rear axle, the greater will be the tendency of the caravan to cut corners.

When towing - take corners wider

The result of this effect is that, when towing, one should take corners, including roundabouts, somewhat wider. In other words, approach the corner from further out in the road.

The other significant point to remember is that your stopping distance when braking is going to be some 20% greater than when driving solo.

You must become familiar with the extra width behind you, and allow for it when overtaking or meeting other traffic. Some caravans are taller than others - be aware of your extra height at such places as filling stations with low canopies, footbridges etc.

On some roll-on, roll-off ferries, not all caravans will fit underneath the mezzanine car decks at the sides of the main vehicle deck. Slightly taller caravans and those with certain rooftop TV aerials need to be loaded in the centre of the main vehicle deck, with the coaches and lorries. The difference in height may only be a few inches or so, but enough to do a fair amount of damage.

I once had to conduct a heated exchange - in French - with a crew member who wanted to put my outfit underneath a mezzanine deck when I knew it would not actually fit. Fortunately the Entente Cordiale and common sense triumphed in the end.

When towing a caravan you are restricted to a speed of 50 mph in the UK *(60 mph maximum on dual carriageways and motorways)*. Do note that these figures represent a legal maximum, not a recommended minimum. Remember also the 85% caravan/car weight advice if you are not experienced in caravan towing.

On the subject of towing speeds, it might be of interest to readers to know that a new world land speed record for a towed caravan was set up in September 1998. Car magazine journalist Mark Walton achieved a speed of 126.8 mph in an 8 cylinder Chrysler Viper towing an Abbey Iona at RAF Alconbury, in near perfect weather conditions.

The Iona was chosen because, being slightly narrower than average, wind resistance was lessened. It was in standard touring trim and, surprisingly, no stabiliser was fitted. The only departure from standard was the fitting of low profile tyres which were rated up to 130 mph. We are not told the noseweight or the weight to which the caravan was ballasted, but it has to be a pretty convincing piece of evidence of the towing stability of the outfit. 126 mph? Don't try it at home.

When towing you must not use the right-hand or lane number 3 of a motorway which has more than two lanes, unless an extra wide load takes up more than one lane.

On a narrow or winding road, do avoid holding up other traffic. On such a road, with a queue of traffic behind you, pull into the side at the first opportunity and let the queue pass you.

When you first set off, keep your speed down until you become accustomed to the feel of the outfit. As a general rule, however, don't drive more slowly than necessary, although you must consider your permitted maximum speed and the principles of general road safety.

Your outfit will be 9 metres long or more, and not easy to overtake quickly. Don't bunch up with traffic in front of you. Leave ample room for larger and faster vehicles to overtake and pull in safely in front of you.

Pairs of caravan outfits in convoy are often guilty of this bad driving fault. If you are holidaying with friends and taking two vans, arrange to meet at your destination. You will find this much

> Keep your speed down until you become accustomed

easier than playing 'follow my leader' and you will certainly cause less danger and aggravation to other road users.

If you must move in pairs don't sit on your buddy's tail. At 50 mph your stopping distance is 175 feet *(or 53 metres)*, not 20 feet. *(Look it up in the Highway Code.)* When towing, add 20% more for safety. True, an emergency stop with a caravan is perfectly feasible, but not really desirable. You don't really want all your cupboard doors to burst open at once.

Two caravan outfits driven close together occupy 80 feet of road or more - difficult for a large lorry to overtake in one bite, and on a single carriageway road, almost impossible. Stay well back and leave ample space between the two outfits so that other vehicles can 'leapfrog' past you in safety.

After missed-altogether and incorrect signals, the next most common serious driving fault must surely be driving too close to the vehicle in front, and is even more hazardous when practised by two caravans in tandem. It's a lunatic philosophy under any circumstances; you don't get to your destination any quicker by tailgating the vehicle in front.

Caravanners, sadly, are often not the 'flavour of the month' with other road users. This is the result of thoughtless and selfish driving on the part of a few. Remember - there is no better lesson than a good example.

> You are sadly not flavour of the month with other road users

Overtaking

If you overtake a slower moving lorry, you may notice in your nearside mirror that the driver flashed his headlights when you had passed. This is to tell you that the rear of your caravan is now clear of the front of the lorry, so you can safely return to your nearside lane. The polite reply is to briefly flash your taillights as a 'thank you' signal, and keep moving. Having passed the lorry, don't slow down and get in its way.

These headlight signals are not to be found in the Highway Code but they are widely practised by drivers of large goods vehicles, and I firmly believe in extending the same courtesy to the driver of a long LGV who overtakes your outfit. Almost invariably you will receive your 'thank you' in response

If you are overtaken at some speed by a particularly large lorry or coach, you are often sucked sideways for an instant and your outfit swings to the right towards the overtaking vehicle. This happens particularly if it is passing you without leaving much room between that vehicle and yours. Don't overreact, don't brake suddenly. Keep a firm hold on your steering wheel and try to ease slightly over to your left. Don't wrench suddenly at your steering wheel, as this will only set up a 'snaking' reaction. It is an unpleasant sensation, but it rights itself within a few seconds. or The main thing is not to be taken by surprise. Constantly use your offside mirror, particularly on motorways, and if you see a large vehicle moving up to overtake, ease into the left to increase the gap between the two outfits.

Snaking occurs when the caravan starts to wag from side to side, eventually wagging the car also. This should rarely occur with an outfit that is not overloaded or badly balanced. If snaking does occur, however, do not brake or accelerate. Lift your foot off the accelerator, let the speed fall away, and stability should soon be restored.

Stabilisers

Snaking inevitably leads on to the subject of stabilisers. The function of a stabiliser is to *(a)* prevent a trailer from wagging from side to side behind the towing vehicle, and *(b)* to prevent the trailer from pitching, which is an up and down vertical movement of the nose of the trailer, which includes a similar up and down movement in the rear of the tow car. This, of course, is not only uncomfortable but adversely affects road holding.

Stabilisers fall mainly into two groups. One is a single blade leaf spring which clamps firmly to the towbar on the car, and the rear end of the blade locates in a bracket or stirrup fastened to the draw bar of the caravan. At the front end of the blade is a damper which contains tightly clamped friction pads which resist any turning movement between car and trailer. This damping device is not sufficient to prevent car and caravan turning a corner, but it effectively damps down any tendency of the trailer to wag or sway from side to side when moving in a straight line. The blade of the leaf spring has two additional functions, in that it counteracts any tendency of the noseweight of the caravan to depress the rear of the tow car, and this same influence counteracts any pitching tendency.

I use a most effective stabiliser of this type marketed by SAS, the caravan security people, which features a quick release device on the friction damper, which makes attaching and detaching the stabiliser much easier. This type of stabiliser does not go on ad infinitum without a service. The fibre pads need replacing and the stabiliser needs the friction surfaces cleaning. Dust and dirt become trapped

If snaking occurs - do not brake or accelerate

2

and compressed between the friction pads and this eventually becomes glazed, resulting in ghastly groaning noises when you are turning a corner, and it is a sure sign that your stabiliser is overdue for a service.

An excellent stabiliser overhaul service is provided by the Stabiliser Clinic. This is run by Jonathan Ward, an expert in his field, who will strip down your stabiliser, clean or replace the friction pads, set the friction pads to the correct tension, and return the stabiliser to you most promptly.

A leaf spring stabiliser with friction pads set at the wrong degree of tightness is virtually useless, and it is a fact that many caravanners are using ineffective stabilisers, not having had them serviced or checked for literally years.

The Stabiliser Clinic can supply you with a testing device plus torque wrench which will enable you to maintain your stabiliser in correct working order.

The bracket or stirrup which is supplied with leaf spring stabilisers has to be attached to the drawbar of the caravan, and at one time, these brackets were bolted to the caravan, which meant drilling a couple of holes in the drawbar.

The Stabiliser Clinic

Holme Grove
By Pass Road
Garstang PR3 INA
Phone: 01995 603745
Mobile: 07970 685766

Brackets are still available for retro or replacement fitting to an older caravan, but today's caravans will have the manufacturer's warranty nullified if the chassis is drilled at any point. Leaf spring stabilisers, therefore, are supplied currently with brackets which clamp around the drawbar member, rather than having to be bolted to it. Do check carefully on your warranty conditions before drilling a hole in a caravan chassis, for any purpose.

Check your warranty before drilling holes in your caravan chasis

A more recent and unconventional device is a stabiliser which does not reply on friction as a damping force.

The 'Straightliner', like the leaf spring stabiliser, attaches to the drawbar of a caravan via a bracket or stirrup which is bolted onto the van chassis, but there the similarity ends. The damping action of the Straightliner is via a gas filled ram/strut in the centre section, which acts to bring the caravan back into line with the car when snaking occurs, and the greater the instability, the greater the corrective force. With a conventional stabiliser, friction tends to resist a side to side movement of the caravan, but the same friction tends to resist the van coming back into line with the car.

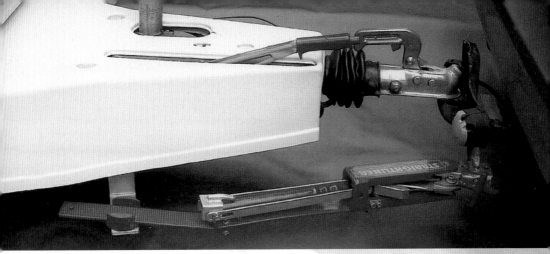

The Straightliner lacks this disadvantage and in addition, there is no resistance to steering when reversing or performing tight manoeuvres. A secondary cam system will disengage the unit when reversing.

Obviously more expensive than friction type units, the Straightliner retails at around £200, but in stringent testing has proved most effective. It is marketed by Safe & Secure Products of Bristol *(SAS)* who will gladly forward details. **See back of the book for Useful Contacts**.

The second type of stabiliser based on friction is simpler in principle to the leaf spring models, but tends to be more expensive. There is no separate gadget to fix between car and trailer, the stabiliser is permanently part of the coupling head on the caravans's drawbar.

The handle which activates the clamp action on the tow ball when pressed down can be clearly seen in the photographs on pages 40 and 41.

When the coupling head is dropped onto the tow ball, a clamp is manually activated which causes the jaws of the coupling head to grip the towball very tightly, and friction between coupling head and towball prevents undue lateral movement

A stabiliser based on friction is simpler than leaf spring models

between the two. With this friction type of stabiliser, the towball must be completely free from grease, unlike the more conventional connection between coupling head and towball.

Al-Ko now offer two sizes of stabiliser coupling head. The SKS 1300 copes with caravans up to 1360 kg in weight, and the AKS

3004 for trailers up to 3,000 kg. The AKS 3004 unit contains four friction pads, as distinct from the two pads in the AKS 1300, which helps to control pitching - a fore and aft motion - as well as snaking.

Similar stabilising coupling heads are the Westphalia, supplied by SAS products of Bristol and another German one, the Winterhof, which is fitted to all Hobby caravans imported into the UK.

Friction pads for Al-Ko stabilisers are designed to have a life of some 50,000 kilometres, and are available as replacements.

These friction stabilisers are inevitably more expensive than the leaf spring type. At the time of writing, the Al-Ko models listed here vary from £255 up to £294 inc. VAT. They are most effective, and can be retro fitted to replace an earlier coupling head.

Friction clamp stabilisers are more expensive than the leaf spring type

When I see towed caravans swaying and snaking from side to side I am surprised that more caravanners don't appreciate the value of a good quality stabiliser. At this point I know that the purists will argue that a correctly loaded van towed by a competent

driver should not need a stabiliser, and there is some merit in this. The point here is that **A STABILISER IS NOT A REMEDY FOR A BADLY LOADED OR OVERLOADED CARAVAN.** It is, however, an essential piece of safety equipment.

To round off this section on stabilisers, the good news is that around 2002/2003, several caravan manufacturers began to fit the Al-Ko friction type stabiliser as standard equipment on certain models, thus cutting out the older type of coupling head.

This trend is spreading rapidly, and the 2004 design year saw many manufacturers fitting either Al-Ko or Winterhof stabiliser/ coupling heads to their entire range. Now, almost all new caravans sold in the UK are fitted with Al-Ko stabilisers.

Bad news for makers of leaf-spring and similar stabilisers, but good news for safer towing all round. For many years, however, there will be a need to retro-fit stabilisers to pre-21st century vans.

An important point to note on both Al-Ko and Winterhof stabilisers is that they project further forward than the basic coupling head, and this often results in there being insufficient space between the towball and the bodywork *(usually the bumper)* of the car, so making it difficult to hitch the caravan onto the car.

Some caravanners have sought to remedy this by using longer bolts to connect the towball to the towing bracket, and using 'spacers' to make the towball stand further away from the car's bumper.

THIS IS A POTENTIALLY DANGEROUS PRACTICE, and is not the remedy. A caravan dealer who sells a van with an Al-Ko type stabiliser has a duty to ensure that the customer's towbar and towball are suitable. A modified towball should be supplied or, if necessary, a complete new towbar. Shortcutting the problem with spacers is unsafe and could invalidate warranty and insurance cover.

A stabiliser is an essential piece of safety equipment

Whilst dealing with the extreme front end of the caravan, another improvement worth noting is that many manufacturers are now also fitting gas assisted handbrakes, which make it much easier to release the handbrake, particularly when it has been applied tightly.

Checklist:

Towing

1 Equip your car with towing mirrors. ✔

2 The speed limit in the UK for towing a caravan is 50 mph on single carriageways, and 60 mph on dual carriageways, including motorways. ✔

3 Don't hold up other, faster traffic. ✔

4 Keep a sensible distance from the vehicle in front, and leave room for others to overtake you. ✔

5 Do get a stabiliser if not already fitted. ✔

6 Remember: good driving, whether towing or not, consists mostly of good manners and common sense. ✔

7 On motorways keep a good lookout behind for the 'heavies'. ✔

Loading - Weight Distribution

Weight distribution is vital in obtaining a stable caravan. A van must be nose-heavy if it is to give a stable, safe, snake-free tow. The accuracy of this noseweight is quite critical and you may well have to experiment. You should aim for something around 70 kgs (154 lbs) or alternatively go for about 7% of the laden weight of the caravan. You should also consult the handbook for the car to see what maximum noseweight of trailer is stipulated. With some cars, this can be quite a limiting factor.

You can buy a simple spring gauge which sits on the ground and you lower the coupling head of the caravan on to it to get a nose-weight reading. Simpler still, use your bathroom scales. Don't stand the jockey wheel on the scales - you won't get a correct reading. Use a short piece of wood directly under the coupling head, making sure the caravan is level and the hand brake applied.

Al-Ko introduced, in 2006, a heavy duty jockey wheel assembley which has a built-it nose load indicator, guaranteed accurate to within 10%. It retails at approx. £90.00. **See _Useful Contacts_**.

Weight distribution is vital

Twenty years ago gas cylinders were carried clamped to the caravan towbar. Ten years later found them still at the front but in a locker, which often carried the spare wheel and even the battery. More recently caravans have had a dedicated gas cylinder locker somewhere along the side of the van, nearer the axle. Front-end gas cylinder stowage used to contribute to excessive noseweight, but in a rear end kitchen, this would be offset by the weight of fridge and oven.

You must experiment with your loading until you know how to distribute your gear. Heavy items such as awnings, awning poles, boxes of food and crates of brown ale should go on the caravan floor near the centre, ie over the axle. Keep most of the weight on the floor or in lockers under the beds. Avoid weight at the rear end of the caravan, which contributes to a tendency to swing from side to side. Don't load up the eye-level cupboards and lockers with heavy items - you want as low a centre of gravity on the caravan as possible. Don't just cram it all in and set off with an overloaded, badly distributed van-full. Plan carefully.

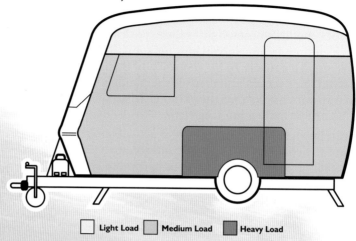

Light Load   Medium Load   Heavy Load

Only recently, on a delightful wooded site in the Vendée region of France, we sat, glass in hand, and watched with growing disbelief as a French couple prepared their caravan for departure. Our interest was first aroused by the spectacle of Madame going carefully over the outside of the awning with a pink feather duster, which drew an unprintable comment from Herself. Madame flaunted ornate dangly earrings and a coloured headscarf, from the periphery of which peeped a couple of curlers. She was every inch your thinking man's Vera Duckworth.

After the treatment with the feather duster, the awning was then collapsed and stowed, with bursts of advice from the contestants in the ongoing game of boules, which seemed to be held all day, every day, on a nearby vacant pitch.

Don't just cram it all in - Plan carefully

With all surplus gear stowed, Monsieur reversed his car to the van and finally wound up his corner steadies. As he raised the last rear steady, the nose of the caravan reared up like some primeval dinosaur, and the van settled on its tail at an angle of 45 degrees to the ground. It was unbelievable.

'Oh la la!' cried Madame. Boules was abandoned, the players swarming round the van, some bearing down on the drawbar, others lifting at the rear.

I dearly wanted a photograph of this spectacle, but of course the camera was in the car, the car was locked and the keys were God knows where.

Meanwhile, with much straining, the coupling head of the caravan was forced down on to the car's towball and latched. The rear of the Renault rose a perceivable two or three inches. The whole operation was volubly directed by the chef de boules, an impressively stout gent in trousers, flip-flops, vest and beret, a Gauloise seemingly glued to the lower lip.

The van sagged visibly at the back. Heaven knows what was loaded into it, but no attempt was made to move it. Electrics were attached, also - give him his due - a stabiliser. Everyone stood back with murmurs of satisfaction. Monsieur and she of the pink feather duster shook hands all round, to cries of 'à l'année prochaine' and 'bonne route', climbed aboard and moved off. Boules was resumed.

We ourselves left a couple of days later, bound for Southern Brittany. We scanned the roadside in vain near the campsite for signs of a totally decimated, tail-heavy French caravan. How the outfit handled on tow one can only imagine. I do know it was the most dangerous piece of caravanning malpractice I think I have ever seen. I do wish I had taken a photograph.

Checklist:

Loading

1 Find the best nose-weight for your outfit - somewhere around 150 lbs (65-70 kg). Check it every time you load up. Don't guess. Aim for about 7% of your laden weight. ✓

2 Keep weighty items down at floor level and amidships (over the axle). ✓

3 Wedge loose items firmly in place. ✓

4 The centre of gravity must be kept low. ✓

5 If you don't need it, don't take it! ✓

6 Check your car's handbook for the maximum permitted noseweight of trailer. DON'T exceed it. ✓

2

Hitching Up

Hooking your loaded caravan on to the car is possibly the next task. Probably you can manfully pick up this 100-150 lb of nose-weight and, with the family pushing the loaded caravan, you can all struggle towards the car, but better still bring the car to the van. The family will not thank you for acquiring a pre-holiday hernia, so leave the caravan where it is - on level ground if possible. Raise up the coupling head at the front of the caravan by winding the jockey wheel stem until the coupling is two or three inches above the height of the towball on the car.

Ask someone to stand by the coupling on the caravan with a hand held up directly over the coupling and high enough to be seem through the rear window of the car. Slowly reverse the car up to the caravan, aiming to position the towball on the car close to the caravan coupling, a few inches to either side of it. This is easy to say, not always easy to do. A good tip is to fix a small piece of white adhesive paper to the inside of the car rear window, dead central from the side to side aspect, right over the towball. Height is not critical - about halfway up the window will do.

You need a similar patch on the inside front caravan window, again dead central. Lining up these two marks in your car rear-view mirror, as you reverse up to the van, enables you easily to position the towball and coupling head within a few inches of each other. Expect a burst of applause from the onlookers.

If the car can be stopped with towball and coupling level, and a few inches to one side of each other, it is a simple matter to swing the front end of the caravan to whichever side is necessary in order to position the coupling directly over the towball on the car. In this position, simply wind down the jockey wheel stem until the caravan coupling locks over the towball. Ensure that the coupling is fully engaged over the towball and locked.

Note that you cannot swing the front of the caravan to either side unless the van handbrake is in 'off' position - or disengaged; hence the desirability of hooking up on level ground. Now reverse-wind the jockey wheel, see the caravan coupling lift the back of the car. This ensures that the coupling is fully locked on to the ball.

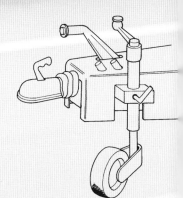

Hitching up
Towball and coupling head

Next, wind the jockey wheel back into its tube, or housing, then unclamp the tube and pull it up as far as it will go, until the jockey wheel itself is located tight up underneath the drawbar, and re-clamp it securely. The wheel is now well clear of the road for towing.

Now attach the safety chain or breakaway cable which we mentioned earlier in the stabiliser section.

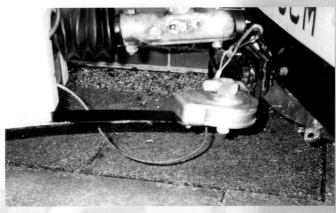

Look at the photograph; The breakaway cable is wrongly attached to the eye above the towing bracket. It should have been passed through the eye and clipped back on to itself. This would correct the other fault, which is the length of slack in the cable. It is obviously too long, to the point where it will drag on the road and suffer excessive wear. This safety chain, or breakaway cable ensures that in the unlikely event of the caravan becoming detached from the car, or the car towball failing, the caravan's handbrake will be applied just prior to the cable failing as the car continues on its way.

Next attach your stabiliser, if applicable, to car and caravan, and finally plug in your electric leads from the van into the 7-pin sockets on the car. *The function of these two 7-pin plugs and sockets is covered in **Chapter 6 - 12 volt electricity**.*

At the time of writing the two types of 7 pin plugs and sockets are rapidly giving way to a single combination with 13 pins, and this is dealt with in more detail in chapter 5 which deals with 12 volt electrics. By mid 2009 Bailey were fitting 13 pin electrics across their whole range.

Having plugged in, get your tireless crew to stand behind the caravan and check all the rear lights as you operate them in the car. Left and right indicators, stop lights, rear and numberplate lights, fog lights and outline marker lights, if fitted and, finally, the forward facing caravan side lights. Remember also to check your hazard lights.

Number One Son, also a caravanner, actually managed to plug the 12N plug into his car socket upside down. Plug and socket have a projection and groove which renders this error virtually impossible, but he managed it. The mistake was discovered when another caravanner, whom he had overtaken earlier, caught him up at a service station and advised him that when he moved to the left his right indicator showed, and when moving right, the left one showed.

Remember to check your hazard lights

2

Ensure all
windows and
doors are
locked

Chris assured the bewildered fellow traveller that this was definitely not intentional, and discovered the upside-down plug. So be warned.

This, incidentally, highlights the need for checking all lights before setting off. Your crew should call out 'left' and 'right' as indicators are tested, not just 'OK'.

On caravans manufactured after October 1990, you will find an extra set of road lights known as 'outline marker lights'. These are now a European Community/British requirement. They are found high up on the sides of a caravan, and show a white light to the front and a red light to the rear, similar to the lights found on the sides of a large lorry.

Before moving off, check that the caravan jockey wheel is fully raised up and clamped firmly, the van handbrake is off, the manual reversing catch *(on old vans)* is released, and the caravan door closed and locked. Before finally closing the van door you should have checked that all the windows are shut and fastened, the roof lights closed, all cupboard and locker doors fastened, and no loose items left to bang about inside the caravan. Ensure that gas cylinders, whether carried in caravan or car, are securely located and in an upright position.

You now have a loaded caravan hooked on to a loaded car. Take a critical look from the side at the attitude of caravan and car. If the van appears nose-down, and the car sits there tail-down and nose-up, then you either have too great a nose-weight on the van or inadequate rear suspension on your car. Riding with car and caravan tilted like this you will severely dazzle oncoming drivers at night, even with dipped headlights, and you will not get the smoothest and safest ride. Some cars *(eg Citroën)* have self-levelling suspension systems which automatically compensate for the effect of caravan nose-weight.

Car suspension aids

There are a number of ways in which to assist, or 'beef up' the rear suspension of a towcar in order to make the noseweight of a trailer more acceptable.

The specialists in this field are Ashley Banks. **See *Useful Contacts*.** They can provide various solutions, depending on the type of suspension on your car, ie leaf springs, trailing arms, coil springs etc. Special shock absorbers, coil springs containing rubber spheres and other devices are available.

Two of our previous towcars had coil springs on the rear suspension, and in each case I bought, from Ashley Banks, a pair of extra coil springs to fit inside the existing coils and these effectively stiffened up the rear suspension to cope easily with the noseweight of the caravan.

Hitching Up

1 Is coupling of caravan securely locked over towball on car? (Most important!) ✓

2 Jockey wheel fully raised and firmly clamped? ✓

3 Handbrake of caravan fully off? ✓

4 Safety chain or breakaway cable secured to car? ✓

5 12 volt electric plugs connected to car sockets? ✓

6 Check that all road lights on caravan are working - particularly indicators. ✓

7 Are all caravan cupboard doors shut and fastened? ✓

8 Roof light(s) closed? ✓

9 Caravan door locked? Keys in your pocket and not still in the van door? ✓

10 Of course you had both car and caravan serviced, tyre pressures checked etc, before setting off. ✓

Finally, in connection with bringing the caravan to the car prior to hitching up, see the section on electric caravan movers. *See Chapter 7 - Equipment and Accessories.*

Unhitching and Levelling

Now, after loading and joining caravan and car, and driving carefully and sensibly, you and your crew arrive at your chosen site. We will talk about the different types of caravan site, both at home and abroad. *See Chapter 8 - Caravan and Camping Sites.*

Let's say you have arrived at a Certificated Location or Certificated Site in a farmer's field. The spot you choose should be as level as possible. Avoid getting to the bottom of a slope, since if it rains heavily the ground may become waterlogged, making it virtually impossible to get the caravan back up again on leaving. Towing, except with a four-wheeled drive vehicle, would be out of the question because of wheel-spin.

Detaching caravan from car is the reverse process of hitching up. Having found your level site, apply the handbrake of the van, detach the electric leads between caravan and car, and remove the stabiliser and breakaway cable. Release the clamp holding the jockey wheel, lower the jockey wheel on to the ground and retighten the clamp. If you wish, you can now manually lift the caravan coupling head clear of the car *(vertebrae permitting)* but in this case you would leave the caravan handbrake off since you will need to swing the nose of the van to one side, once it is clear of the car's towball. Better still, raise the caravan coupling head by winding the jockey wheel handle until the coupling is raised clear of the towball, then move the car away.

> Consider the view from the front end - where you usually sit for meals etc

Towing on to blocks

Do not forget to replace the towball cover immediately, otherwise as soon as someone goes to unload the car boot they will get grease from the towball on their legs unless you have an Al-Ko friction type coupling head, in which case your towball will be dry and free from grease.

Before detaching caravan from car you should consider which way you want it to face. Primarily you would consider the view from your caravan's front end, which is where you usually sit for meals etc. If you are also rigging an awning, the prevailing wind might be a consideration.

You may, of course, be on a more organised site than a farmer's field, and you could be required to site your caravan in the same way as your neighbour's. If you are on level ground, turning the caravan around only needs a bit of push on the part of your family or perhaps helpful neighbours. Remember, though, that you cannot swing the caravan round with the handbrake applied.

Having positioned the caravan, you wind down the corner steadies until the caravan rests firmly on all four corners. The steadies aren't designed to lift the wheels off the ground, but just to take some of the load and, as the word implies, to keep the caravan from rocking in a wind.

A useful purchase is a small plastic triangle into which are set two spirit levels at right angles to each other. With this placed on a flat surface inside the caravan, you can adjust the corner steadies until the caravan is level, both side to side and fore and aft.

Your caravan should be positioned level for reasons of both personal comfort and technical necessity. For example, sleeping with the feet higher than the head induces a pounding in the ears, and rolling out of bed makes for a disturbed night anyway.

For technical reasons a level van is a must since if you're more than five degrees out, the fridge won't function. It can also produce the strange effect, on washing dishes, of water from the dripping plates running 'uphill' to the wrong end of the draining board, and thence into the cupboard containing the corn flakes. This phenomenon tends to prompt some flak from Head Office, and she could well add a load of verbal about forward planning.

If the ground slopes from one side of the caravan to the other, before detaching caravan from car you must tow it up on to some wooden blocks placed in front of the downhill wheel. **See below.**

Your caravan should be positioned level for many reasons.

Towing on to blocks

2

I always carry one or two 8-inch long pieces of 4-inch x 2-inch or 4-inch x 3-inch timber to cope with sloping sites. You also need to carry four pieces of plank, ½-inch or ¾-inch thick, each about 6 inches long by 3 inches wide. These are to go under the corner steadies to prevent them sinking into the ground when you site the caravan.

If you have cause to tow one wheel up on to blocks or a ramp, make sure that, having done so, you firmly place a chock behind EACH wheel, rather than relying on the caravan's handbrake.

Position the van using the car - it saves money with the osteopath

A useful tip in this connection concerns reversing onto a pitch. We know that reversing a modern caravan will automatically disengage the van brakes, so if you reversed onto a pitch, before unhitching, just draw forward a few inches or so, otherwise the van brakes could remain disabled, making your handbrake ineffective.

It's convenient to place your spirit level on the plastic fairing which covers the drawbar at the front of the van, whilst you tweak the corner steadies, but do first be sure that the surface of the fairing is in the same plane as the rest of the caravan. If it isn't, you'll have to think again. On the shelf inside the front window is a convenient spot.

You will have to experiment.

So far then in this chapter we've got you a car which suits your caravan, you have a caravan whose size and layout suits your family and whose weight safely matches the towcar. You know how to hook the van up to the car and you're getting the hang of towing on the road, that is to say `forwards', right? So far so good.

Now the next chapter deals with how to reverse a caravan, or as they say round our way 'mek it ger back'ards duck.'

In case you form the opinion that everyone living above Grantham has got webbed feet, let me assure you that 'duck' is a form of greeting or accolade bestowed on all and sundry, regardless of class, creed or ethnic origin.

Once you have mastered the reversing business, we shall have dealt with most of the complicated stuff to do with caravanning.

Up to this point it has all been about things which you have got to deal with yourself, the rest of the book mostly describes what the caravan manufacturers have done for you to make life comfortable.

At the end of the next chapter we'll tell you how everything you've read so far can be gone over and demonstrated in detail on an excellent day's course, including how to mek it ger back'ards, so read on.

unhitching and levelling

1 Get the van positioned using the car - it's easier than pushing it (see Chapter 3 on reversing).

2 Choose the site carefully: prevailing wind: position of sun: view: level: firm ground if possible: access: exit

3 Tow one wheel on to wood blocks to level, if necessary.

4 Before unhitching van from car, jockey wheel must be down and clamped, and the caravan handbrake in'on' position especially if one wheel is up on blocks. Detach stabiliser, electrics and breakaway cable. Finally detach caravan from car, and move car away.

5 Replace car towball cover immediately - or get greasy legs.

6 Do not use corner steadies as jacks; they are to steady the caravan, not take the total weight.

7 Get the van level.

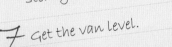

Reversing and Manoeuvring

3

So now we come to the oft-dreaded subject of reversing and manoeuvring. How easy it looks when you watch the skilled LGV driver reversing a 45-foot articulated lorry into a loading bay. Well the simple truth is that it is easier to reverse a big articulated lorry than a car and caravan, and I've done both.

It's easier to reverse an articulated lorry

An articulated lorry has a short tractor and a long trailer which makes for easier reverse steering, whereas a car and caravan are often the same length as each other. The extreme is reached when you try to reverse a little 5 cwt camping trailer which is much shorter than the car. Don't try to practise reversing with such a set-up – the result is really discouraging. It 'jack-knifes' very easily.

Reversing to the Left

The first thing to grasp is that if you have caravan and car in a straight line, fore and aft, and you want to swing the back of the van round to the left while reversing, you must first turn the steering wheel to the **right**, ie the opposite of the normal drill for reversing the car solo.

■ ***Below:*** *Figure 1 - Reversing to the left*

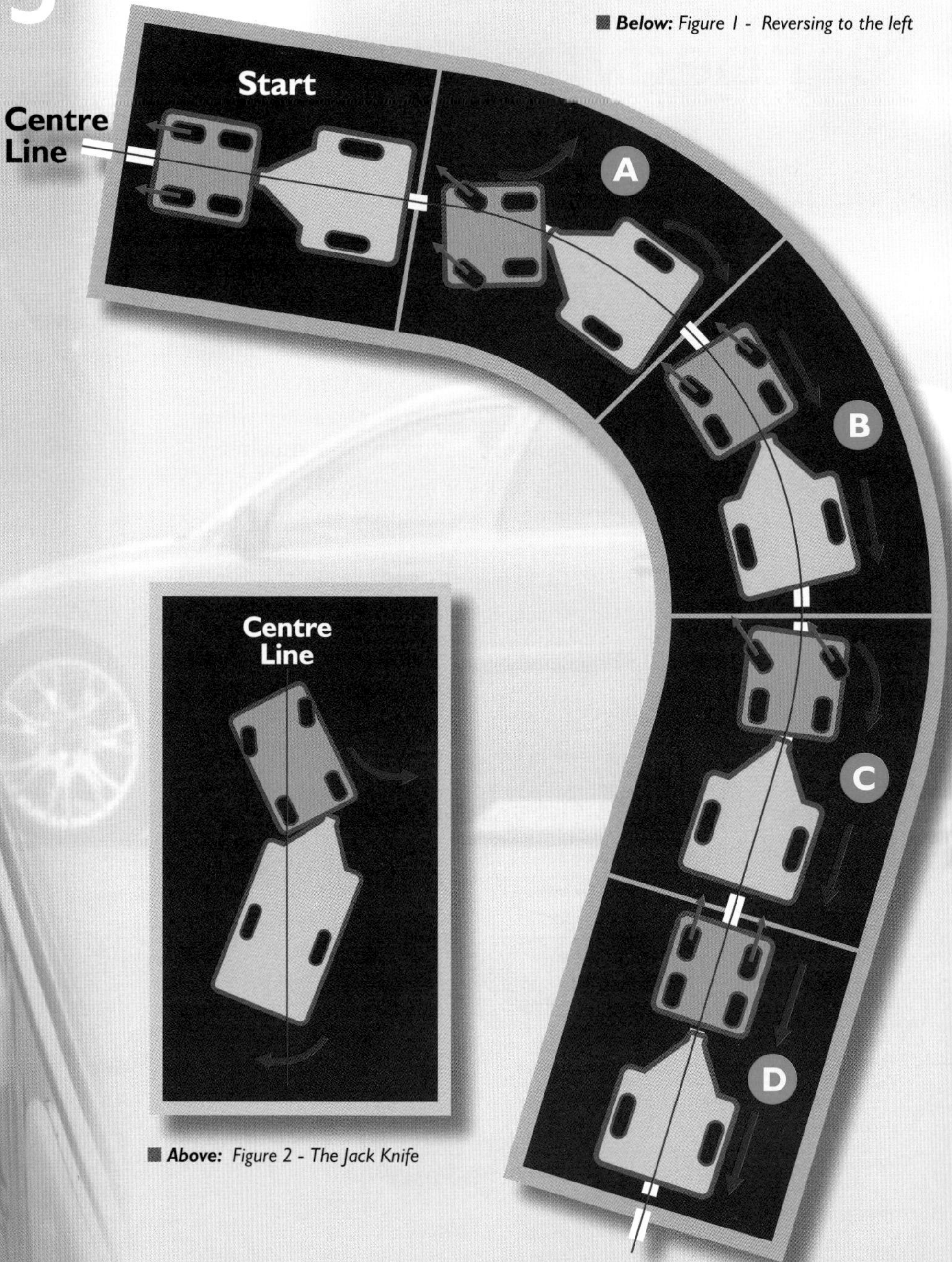
Start
Centre Line
A
B
C
D
Centre Line

■ ***Above:*** *Figure 2 - The Jack Knife*

The reason for this is as follows. On turning the steering wheel to the **right**, the back of the car *(and towball)* will swing to the **right** of the centre line, pushing the nose of the caravan also to the **right** of the centre line. The caravan will then pivot about its axle, and the rear of the caravan will swing to the **left** *(see Figure 1(A))*, which is what we are trying to achieve.

This is where disaster usually strikes, for if you keep the wheel to the right too long you will have the rear of the car and the front of the caravan both too far to the **right**. A little further like this and car and caravan will jack-knife, with the left side of the drawbar hard up against the left-hand rear end of the car *(as in Figure 2)*, with both vehicles too far off the centre line, one to each side.

If we go back to Figure 1(**A**), with the vehicles in the attitude shown, and immediately turn the steering wheel back to the left – not too much – we arrive at a situation as shown in (**B**). Here the car is describing a gentle arc about the now curved centre line. The car is pushing the caravan with the front wheels at just the correct angle to maintain the curve. With very slight adjustments of the steering wheel you can maintain this curve until you have swung the whole outfit round as far as you want – perhaps through 90 degrees.

You must ensure that the angle between car and caravan does not increase, as it will if you tend to straighten the steering wheel, in which case you will again jack-knife *(as in Figure 2)*. This is because with the front wheels centred, the car will not follow our curve but the rear end will move over to the **right** of the curve. This will push the front of the caravan to the **right** of the curve, so that the rear of the van swings to the **left** of the curve and you collapse the outfit *(as in Figure 2)*.

Now the opposite of this last sequence is needed to straighten the outfit out, and run back in a straight line.

Assume we have curved round as far as we want to go *(moving as in (B))*, and we wish to go back in a straight line, as in the 'Start' figure. Turn the steering wheel further to the **left**. *(This may take some believing since we're trying to straighten up – but be patient).* You can see from (**C**) that this swings the front of the car out to the *right* of our curved centre line; **immediately** the front of the car has swung far enough to the right to be in a straight line with the caravan, turn the steering wheel to the right, back to **dead centre** as in (**D**). You are then running back again in a straight line.

> With slight adjustments you can swing the whole outfit round as far as you want

Reversing to the Right

Reversing to the right is just the opposite of the sequences shown in **figure I** - *Page 56*.

Your side mirrors are essential to manoeuvring. As you go back in a straight line you should see equal amounts of caravan in each mirror. If you get an increased amount of van in your **Right** mirror and it begins to disappear from your left mirror, turn the steering wheel slightly to the **Right**. This will immediately correct the swing, but once the outfit is straight you must centre the wheel again. When reversing in a straight line, failure to correct the beginning of a swing *(ie when the caravan gets more prominent in one mirror or the other)* will soon result in a jack-knife.

Correcting a Jack-knife

Now finally how to get out of a jack-knife, or any situation where the caravan is more to one side of the car then you intend. This is unbelievably simple. Stop, and go forward, centralising the steering wheel as you go. The car goes forward in a straight line, and quite simply the caravan follows. After literally a few yards your outfit is in a dead straight line, and you can get back to your intended manoeuvre.

Reversing in a Straight Line

Remember when reversing in a straight line, go slowly, and whichever side of the caravan appears to increase in your mirrors, turn the wheel towards that side. Practise a bit on the flat open ground or in a field. Try going straight back to begin with, using the above formula; then, using a few empty cans or whatever, mark out a gentle curve and try your hand at this. You will soon get the hang of it – particularly if you can practise without an audience! It is very satisfying to be able to arrive on a site and put your caravan where you actually want it, and it really isn't difficult.

Automatic Reversing

When the towcar slows down fairly sharply the caravan tends to 'catch up' with the car, thus pushing the coupling head and draw bar in towards the van, and it is this motion which applies the caravan brakes.

If you reverse the car, you push the draw bar back towards the van, but on a modern caravan, this does NOT apply the van brakes as you would expect. An automatic mechanism in the braking system prevents this happening when a reversing manoeuvre commences.

3

It may take some beleiving but be patient

On a pre-1980 caravan, however, you would have to get out of the car, and apply a reversing catch on the draw bar to prevent the car pushing the draw bar back and applying the caravan brakes.

Practical Caravan Handling Courses

Both the Caravan Club and the Camping and Caravanning Club run practical caravan handling courses for members at weekends at various locations throughout the country. In the case of the Camping and Caravanning Club, these are recognised by the Institute of Advanced Motorists. See *Chapter 9*.

Detailed hands-on instruction is given on hitching up and unhitching, forward and reversing skills, invaluable advice on vehicle and trailer weights and correct load distribution.

The instructors on these Club handling courses are all experienced caravanners and experienced instructors. For some time I was one myself. They are extremely helpful, infinitely patient, and during the course of the day you will find they will cover practically everything we have discussed in this chapter.

It is time well spent, and you will come away with your confidence in handling a caravan enormously improved.

You will soon get the hang of it

Checklist:

Reversing

1 To reverse in a straight line use the side mirrors. On whichever side the caravan seems to show more, turn the steering wheel towards that side. ✓

2 To reverse round to the LEFT, start by turning the steering wheel to the RIGHT. ✓

3 Don't give up. Practise! (And do the handling and manoeuvring course). ✓

One product, One process, Onedrywash

new motorcar

1nedrywash
no water required

CAR CLEANING KIT
will Drywash up to 7

new motorhome

1nedrywash
no water required

MOTORHOME CLEANING KIT
will Drywash up to 4 motorhomes

new caravan

1nedrywash
no water required

CARAVAN CLEANING KIT
will Drywash up to 4 vans

All kits contain:
500ml e Onedrywash
2 micro fibre cloths
2 latex gloves

Onedrywash is available from all caravan or camping outlets – in case of difficulty locating our products, please email our distributor on sales@groveproducts.co.uk for details of your local outlet

Freephone 0800 8818062 or visit www.onedrywash.com

Motor Homes 4

The earlier editions of the book were essentially about caravans and we said in an opening chapter to this edition that much that is written about caravans also applied to motor homes.

At this point, however, it would be appropriate to devote some thought to features which are specific to motor homes.

Early motor homes were really just a commercial panel van with a gas ring and a couple of beds, but they have evolved today into a luxury caravan with an engine.

Who first thought of camping in a commercial van and, exactly when, is not really clear. It must go back 50 years or more to the 1950s. Who does not remember the air-cooled engine early VWs, often pained orange and white, with the chunky spare wheel bolted on the front? Some are still going strong and have now acquired icon status and can command large sums of money like, say, a bull-nosed Morris car.

Back then it was all to do with purchase tax, the forerunner of VAT. Commercial vans, the Ford Transit of the day, were free of purchase tax, but cutting a couple of windows in the side made them liable for tax. Comparing these early motor homes with today's luxury versions is the equivalent of comparing a Tiger Moth with a Boeing 747.

We did say in an earlier chapter that many features in a modern motor home are common to both caravans and motor homes. Many well known motor homes are produced by long-established caravan manufacturers eg. Bessacar, Elddis etc. and this is perhaps the point to look at just what a modern motor home has to offer, and how it can include some of the features of a top quality caravan.

Many features are common to caravans and motor homes

4

There are areas where a motor home is a better bet than a caravan and vice versa. A motor home is more compact making it cheaper to travel on a ferry, it is easier to drive and manoeuvre. It may legally be driven faster, is probably cheaper to insure than a car plus caravan outfit.

Against a motor home it is a nuisance when you want to nip into the town for a meal, or go to the beach or anywhere else for that matter. With a caravan, just lock it up and move off in the car without having to put every loose item in the van stowed away. It is now becoming popular to tow a small car vehind the motor home on a rigid tow, but you are now talking some serious money. A sizeable motor home can often have a 'garage' a large cupboard accessed from outside the motor home, which will accommodate a motor scotter or a number of bicycles, usually under the bed area.

A motor home is easier to drive

If you want to tour all the European capital cities or drive from New York to San Francisco, spending just a couple of nights in one location and there are just the two of you, then a motor home is the ideal answer. A flock of children needs a caravan where you can attach an awning for extra space. I know there are multi bed motor homes, where the most junior member of the crew sleeps in a cramped berth over the driver's cab, but this is not ideal. At the end of the holiday all a motor home becomes is a second car, and a bulky, difficult to park second car it is.

Cost is a factor. You can get a pre-owned two-berth motor home in reasonable nick for around £13,000; a comparable caravan would be around £5,000. If buying new, the gap gets wider.

4

A golden
handshake
often leads
to a motor
caravan

Aside from the American-style motor home with mains voltage generator, two lots of air conditioning and an 8-litre engine, *(these are the size of a long-distance luxury coach and cost £75,000 plus)* you will still find that quite a lot of money is involved. Leaving out the very modest versions which are really an 8-cwt commercial van with a bed and a gas stove, a comfortably appointed motor home with toilet and washing facilities, decent kitchen, fridge and so on is going to cost £30,000-£40,000 or more. For this sort of outlay one could buy a very confortable caravan and a respectable car to tow it with.

There are now a large number of motor home manufacturers in this country and Europe, some of whom are also caravan manufacturers. Sales have exploded in recent years - many dealers put this down to an increase in early retirement or redundancies. The couple concerned want a compact, easy to manage mobile home. Their family have grown up and gone, a two-berth is all they need, and a motor home is where the golden handshake goes.

Caravanners and motor home buffs will argue the relative merits *ad infinitum.* A motor home is less effort - only needing winding down rear corner steadies and levelling up.

Very great strides have been made in recent years in the design and comfort of motor caravans. The earlier ones were really commercial vehicles with a couple of beds and a gas ring, and tended to be produced by commercial vehicle manufacturers. Nowadays, however, caravan manufacturers are leaving their unmistakable mark on motor homes. Firms like Swift, Elddis and

4

**Consider
your type
of holiday**

Auto-Trail are producing vehicles which are less like commercial vans with beds and more like luxury caravans with engines. German imports such as Hymer are well designed and very popular. The current crop of motor caravans or motor homes are thoughtfully designed and beautifully appointed.

This would be an appropriate point at which to list some of the features found in a well designed motor home. As we have already seen, among them are also items found in caravans.

Sizes vary and so, of course, do both diesel and petrol engines. Thatcham approved immobilisers, comfortable swivel cab seats, on board fresh and waste water tanks, fixed double beds, extra (claustrophobic) beds over the cabin, large panoramic opening roof windows, cruise control, reversing sensor, microwave ovens, flat screen TV, mains electric hookups, bas and mains powered climate contol and water heaters, elegant bathrooms with toilet and shower, air conditioning, dual fuel cooking (gas and electric hobs), automatic gear boxes, all these are features of some motor homes.

Not all motor homes have all these goodies and looking at the list one can see where the money goes, and as we said earlier, one can spend a lot of loot on a motor home. And when some of the above features are teamed with a Mercedes chassis and a six-speed gearbox one can see why the result can be expensive.

The Society of Motor Manufacturers and Traders now has a motor home section, and has also formulated a code of practice for this specialised area. The attention to both safety and quality

will be as carefully maintained and regulated as it is in the caravan manufacturing trade. Certainly their products today embody some excellent standards of design and build.

When you decide to embark on a form of nomadic self-sufficiency, a motor home merits as much consideration as a touring caravan.

The same principles apply. Consider what you can afford, to what use you want to put it, and how it would adapt to your family, your many and varied circumstances and your type of holiday.

Caravan Awnings

5

The subject of awnings was mentioned in *Chapter 1*, when discussing your choice of caravan.

Provision of Additional Space

If you have a family I will repeat the advice to consider sleeping a couple of children – or adults – in an awning. This is a better consideration than buying a really large van to sleep everybody, which would be heavy, more expensive and need a bigger car to tow it.

Even with a modest two-berth caravan, an awning can provide a spare bedroom. You would, of course, have an amicably prearranged system of signals, eg a gentle tap on the shoulder means **'you're snoring my Darling'**; two sharp shakes means **'you're still bloody well snoring'**; and three violent shoves means **'for God's sake push off and snore in the awning'**. It's just like being at home really.

Awnings are often available second-hand, either as a separate item or as part of the equipment that goes with a second-hand caravan.

Good value second-hand awnings are often to be seen advertised privately in the various caravan magazines. A couple of pages further on we will discuss how to make sure you get the correct size awning for your caravan.

> An awning can provide a spare bedroom

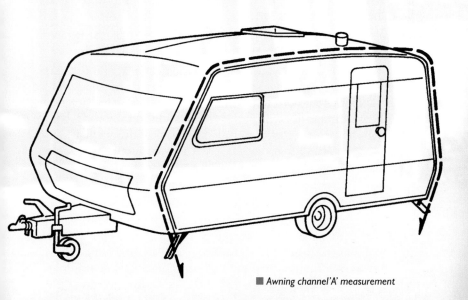

■ *Awning channel 'A' measurement*

Awnings come in many forms, sizes and materials. In recent years porch awnings have become popular and, as the name implies, they are fairly small and are rigged over the caravan door. Only a few feet in width and depth, they nevertheless provide weatherproof storage for folding chairs, welly boots, beach gear and so forth.

Original awnings were made of cotton canvas

A full size awning, ie one that is the same length as the caravan will at least double the amount of floor area available in the van.

The original awnings were made of cotton canvas, and there are still some in use, but great strides have been made in weatherproof synthetic fabrics for both tents and awnings. Acrylic and polyester have the advantage of being quick drying and virtually rot-proof. They will, however suffer from mildew if packed away when wet or damp, so if you have to strike camp with a wet awning, it should be spread and dried as soon as possible.

Construction

Caravans are fitted with an awning rail, which is an alloy channel fitted to the nearside of the caravan, running up one end, along the top and down the other end. The edge of the awning which joins the caravan finishes in a seam which contains a plastic beading, to form a bolt-rope, and this is fed at one end into the end of the channel, and pulled right through around the caravan. This forms a secure and weatherproof joint between awning and van.

The awning rail, or channel, can become distorted if given a knock, and it then becomes difficult or even impossible to feed the fabric of the awning through the channel. I must confess to having distorted the awning channel in the past, when negotiating a particularly narrow entrance, and catching the side of the caravan on an unyielding gatepost.

Restoring the alloy channel to its original profile can be a tedious business, but it is made much simpler by a small gadget called an awning rail spreader. This is one of a wide range of useful caravan accessories produced by W4 Ltd. **See *Useful Contacts* at the back of the book**. It is widely available from caravan dealers' accessory shops.

The awning is supported on a simple framework of poles, which can be of steel, alloy or even fibreglass to reduce weight. Clear plastic film windows, walls which roll up or zip out altogether, and small annexes to contain a chemical toilet are all available features, and of course space depends on the depth of the awning. Several makes of awning can provide a zip-on annexe at one end to provide an extra bedroom.

On most modern caravans there is an outside 12-volt light on the outside wall of the van above the door and so illumination at night in the awning is no problem.

Plastic groundsheets in a variety of sizes are available; these are virtually an impermeable plastic sheet. The drawback to these is that, if left in situ for several days, they have an adverse effect on the grass underneath, tending to turn it yellow. A recent development in awning 'carpets' has considerably improved on this. Many caravan dealers' accessory shops sell carpets or groundsheets which are not completely impermeable, but are an open weave of synthetic strands which allow the carpet to 'breathe', causing less damage to grass. These floor coverings are available in a range of colours and sizes to fit a variety of awnings, and they are usually sold by the running metre off a roll which is about 8 feet wide.

Awning Sizes

Make sure you buy an awning which fits your van. They are loosely described as 'fit 12 – 13 foot van' which narrows things down a little, but the final measurement is important. This is known as the 'A' measurement, and it is the distance from the ground at one end of the caravan, vertically up through the awning channel, around the top of the van and down to the ground again at the other end. **See diagram on page 65**.

Make sure you buy an awning which fits your van

This is easily and accurately obtained by feeding a piece of string from the ground, up around the channel, and then measuring the string. This measurement is usually in centimetres, and for a 12-foot caravan will be something like 750–775 centimetres. It is important to get the measuring correct, since a 12-foot caravan is a 12-foot caravan, but the height of it can vary somewhat between different makes and so, therefore, can the ground-to-ground circumference. It is no good having a 6-inch gap between the ground and the bottom of the awning walls near the caravan.

The 'A' measurement should be taken with the van on level ground, and the corner steadies wound down.

Erecting
an awning
is usually a
two-man
excercise

Erecting the Awning

Before introducing the framework of poles the usual drill is to feed the bolt rope *(the edge of the awning which joins to the caravan)* through the awning channel on the caravan.

Make sure you feed in the correct end first, depending on whether you feed from the front of the van or the rear, otherwise you will find you have the awning inside out. If the end walls and roof of the awning are all in one piece, the whole thing must be fed through the channel at once. If end walls and roof are separate from each other, feed the roof section into the channel first, then erect the framework of poles and finally attach the end walls. This is done by means of sturdy zip-fasteners.

To ease the passage of the awning through the alloy channel, spray the inside of the channel with liquid furniture polish - but NOT detergent. The awning will slide through much more easily.

Alternatively, an awning rail lubricant is available from caravan dealers' accessory shops. There is also a useful little special brush for keeping the awning rail free from dust, gunge and spiders, all of which hinder the easy passage of the awning through the rail.

In any event, erecting an awning is nearly always a two-man job. When first attaching the fabric to the caravan, one person feeds the bolt-rope into the channel while the other pulls the fabric along, and it is here that it is usually necessary to gain some extra height by standing on the caravan step.

When the fabric is in place, either the whole awning or just the roof if the end walls are separate, one person holds up the roof from inside, while the other nips nimbly about, also inside, erecting the framework of poles.

The awning is finally secured by fastening down around the bottom edge with tent pegs. Normally, additional guy-ropes are not necessary, but these are a wise precaution in very windy conditions. If you site your outfit, perhaps at the coast where there is a strong prevailing wind, it is worth arranging things so that the awning is on the sheltered side of the caravan. In these conditions a stone wall or a clump of bushes can make an effective windbreak.

Include a mallet or a hammer in your tool kit – on some types of ground, tent pegs take some knocking in. They are available in either plastic or steel. Many sites now have hard standing pitches. Steel pegs rather than plastic are essential on these.

Finally, a word on poles. On new awnings the poles will collapse down into short lengths on spring-loaded connections. In the case of second-hand poles, some may have perhaps parted company from their neighbouring section, so you have a number of short sections that don't seem to have a home. Even on a new awning where the pole joints are intact, this bag-full of poles lies on the ground in a meaningless jumble, defying you to assemble them without having several bits left over.

Reference to the maker's handout may or may not help. These instructions often seem to be written by someone specially recruited from a Government 'confusing pamphlet' department. More than once, with a new awning, we have stood in a field,

Include a mallet or hammer in your tool kit

longing for a drink, surrounded by a jumble of defiant looking poles, while it steadily grew dark and began to rain, but we usually won in the end.

The moral is to get the dealer, or previous owner, to show you how the poles assemble. The three *(or more)* horizontal poles supporting the roof of the awning have to join with the sidewall of the caravan at the top, just underneath the awning rail on the caravan.

This is either achieved with rubber 'sucker' cups attached to the end of the poles, or by solid plastic hooks on the pole ends which engage with plastic eyes screwed onto the caravan wall.

'Sucker' cups adhere well to a smooth aluminium caravan wall, but not to a wall which has a 'crimpled' surface. This is not important, since there should be tape sewn to the awning roof which ties around the poles, adequately supporting them.

If the awning roof poles are fitted with plastic hooks, remember that holes drilled into the caravan wall, to fix the locating eyes, must be sealed with a waterproof mastic.

When you put the awning up for the first time, identify each section of frame and identify it by writing on a piece of masking tape stuck to the pole. Once familiar with the poles, you should part-assemble them, and lay them out on the ground around the intended site for the awning, where each one will be required, ie left side, right side, front etc. Do this even before you feed the fabric into the awning channel. All this is not nearly as difficult as it sounds, and once you've done it a couple of times it becomes very simple.

There are
18 or more
awnings
available

We used to get our awning up reasonably quickly and, by the time I had pegged down the walls, Herself would produce a pot of tea and the tentative suggestion that perhaps the whole outfit might be better off just a couple of yards further to the right?

There are now some 18 or so different makes of caravan awnings available in the UK, British, Continental and Scandinavian in origin. These contribute a good representative cross section of what is available, and there should be something to suit the most discerning caravanner.

STOP PRESS

While compiling this book, I stumbled on something new and radical that seemed likely to change the whole concept of caravan awnings. Hence this postcript, which will probably seem to be at odds with some of the preceding pages of this chapter.

In the January 2005 edition of **Practical Caravan**, editor Alex Newby wrote in her editorial column. . .

"In an age when we can create a tent that will go up in four minutes, it's hard to believe that many modern *(caravan)* awnings are still so heavy, take around an hour to put up and leave you exhausted before you've even started your holiday, which is why I'm so excited by the new awning from Sunncamp pictured on page 29.

Not only does it look bang up to date but it can be erected in ten minutes flat and costs just a fraction of other porch awnings."

I turned promptly to page 29 and saw this photograph of the Sunncamp Scenic porch.

The following day, I drove a 300 mile round trip to visit the Sunncamp showrooms in Essex. I had a good look at the Scenic, and liked what I saw. *(Sunncamp is the camping division of Sunnflair Ltd.)*

I had a good look at the Scenic, and liked what I saw

Look at any modern dome or igloo tent, regardless of size, and it will not be propped up from inside by heavy, rigid poles like a caravan awning. No, it will be SUSPENDED from lightweight, flexible, fibreglass poles, and Sunncamp have done just that with the small Scenic porch awning. The whole unit fits into a valise no bigger than a sports bag, and weighs less than just the poles of a conventional porch awning.

The unit comprises lightweight Polyester fabric, mesh side vents, deep mud walls and front and sides which zip out. The framework consists of three long flexible fibre poles which are attached, through loops or

5

sleeves, to the OUTSIDE of the awning, as the illustration shows. The poles are made up of short sections, only slightly thicker than a pencil, each with a male and female end, simple and quick to assemble.

Caravan dealers had most encouraging reactions to the Scenic, as a result of which the Scenic Plus soon followed.

Sizes and prices? Well, the small Scenic measures 1.9m wide x 1.8m deep *(6'4" x 6' approx)*. The Scenic Plus measures 2.75m wide x 2.90m deep *(9' x 6'6" approx)*. Both models are 2.4m high *(8' approx)* and will fit caravans between 240 - 255cms high.

Retail prices were quoted as around £129 for the Scenic and £159 for the Scenic plus, but these can vary, since many caravan dealers are open to a bit of a haggle.

Using the same principle of applying modern tent technology to awnings, there is a still larger model - the Contempo. This is a slightly different shape, but while still not a full awning, it measures an impressive 3m wide x 2.8m deep *(10' x 9'4" approx)*, which makes it a whopping big porch. Suggested retail price is £169.

After 18 successful months with the Scenic and Scenic Plus, Sunncamp took the 'igloo' style construction a stage further, and at the February 2006 Show at the NEC they launched the Ultima, a truly radical shape in porch awnings, with a suggested retail price of £180.

Having a 'lean-to' appearance, the Ultima looks more like a full awning than a porch, depending on the size chosen - either 260cm or 390cm wide. Both versions are 240cm deep, but depend on 260 or 390 cms of level awning rail, since if the awning rail dips down at the ends, the awning will not sit correctly.

This lightweight modern tent technology cannot be applied to full awnings, only the caravan roof section of awning rail is involved, not the vertical end sections.

How do these lightweights cope with heavy weather? Well, reports indicate that they have withstood some pretty fierce storms and winds. The two Scenics each come with a pair of double guy ropes, the big Contempo with two pairs. All guy ropes are in a sturdy, bright fluorescent yellow nylon, to avoid tripping over.

This was a totally new concept of caravan awnings, and at a fraction of the price, a fraction of the weight and erectable in minutes, it is already a winner.

Awnings withstand pretty fierce storms

Sunnflair Ltd
Cutlers Road
South Woodham Ferrers
CHELMSFORD
Essex CM3 5XJ
Tel: 01245 329933

Colour catalogues are available from most caravan dealers.
See *Useful Contacts*.

Checklist:

Awnings

1 Know the size required. The vital statistic is the ground-to-ground measurement - in centimetres. (Ground level, up around the awning rail or channel on the caravan, and back to ground level). ✓

2 Synthetic fabrics are more practical than cotton. ✓

3 Identify and label with masking tape the sections of frame. ✓

4 Make up some extra guy-ropes with really sturdy pegs, or earth anchors, for really stormy weather. ✓

5 Invest in a groundsheet, or 'breathable' floor covering. ✓

6 Do dry and air thoroughly as soon as possible if the awning has been packed away when wet or even damp ✓

Caravan Awnings 73

Dome Tents • Trailer Tents • Caravan Awnings
Motor Awnings • Accessories

Essential Services

Water Supply Systems

This section on water refers to caravans. The great majority of motor homes have built in fresh water tanks plus waste (or 'grey') water tanks. Most club and commercial camp sites have a dedicated fresh and waste water points.

However you dispense water in your caravan, you've got to get the water to the van in the first place. How do you do this? Well, it depends how far you have to go to fetch it. A really upmarket site may well have a water point for every pitch, or a simple 5-van-only site may have only one tap and it could be a quarter of a mile away. We have been in beautiful, almost deserted locations which were so basic that I had to fetch water in the car. This was a small price to pay for the tranquillity and view.

What do you carry the water in? Well, the larger the container, the less often you go for a refill. On the other hand, the larger it is, the heavier it is. I am constantly amazed by the weird things folk fetch water in – little plastic jugs and items that are so small that all the water is gone after two pots of tea.

Don't carry water, wheel it

The message is: don't carry water, wheel it. There are two main ways of doing this. We use two rectangular 5-gallon plastic jerricans with screw stoppers. Anything bigger than this is too heavy to lift, since 5 gallons weighs 50 lb. If you want to convert this to litres and kilos, feel free. Either way, it's extremely heavy.

Now we don't hump these 50-lb loads about by hand, they go on a neat little two-wheeled trolley which is very easy to trundle and folds flat when not in use. The waste container of our cassette toilet also fits on the trolley, which makes for easier emptying.

You do need two of these 5-gallon containers, since Murphy's Law dictates that when one container runs dry you are inevitably in the middle of washing up, having a shower or whatever. You don't want

■ *Above: Aquaroll fresh water container*

to trail across the site for a refill at that moment; it's easier to get Herself to nip outside and switch the submersible pump to the full container. *(Cries of protest from the anti-chauvinist pig brigade. Actually she enjoys changing the water over.)*

The other type of water container is illustrated. A round drum which has a clip-on handle, it is pulled along like a garden roller. The one illustrated is the Aquaroll which, like the 5-gallon plastic jobs and the wheeled trolley, can be bought from most accessory shops. There are two sizes available, holding either 40 litres or 29 litres *(approx. 9 or 6 gallons)*, but you still need two of them for the aforementioned logistic reasons. Note that they are heavier, bulkier to stow and more expensive than the plastic jerricans.

Waste Containers

If you feed water into your caravan, most of it has to come out again. You will need one or more waste containers, depending on how many waste outlets your van has, usually either two or three.

Waste containers are much like the 5-gallon fresh water containers, ie rectangular and plastic. The waste outlets from the kitchen sink and toilet compartment washbasin are located just underneath the van and a few inches in from the outside edge. A short length of plastic pipe or hose connects the waste spout or spouts to the container.

It is surprising how quickly the waste containers fill up due to washing up, personal ablutions etc. An organised caravan site will have wastewater disposal facilities. Use them, don't just dump it on the nearest patch of grass. Your folding two-wheel trolley comes in useful here. Alternatively the Aquaroll people make an excellent wheeled wastewater trolley to fit under the caravan – capacity 38 litres *(approximately 8 gallons)*.

As an alternative to 2 plastic waste jerricans the wheeled wastemaster is now much more common.

The Wastemaster has a very shallow profile, making it easy to use on a sloping site, where there is little clearance between the ground and the waste outlet at the rear end of the caravan. Another useful feature of the Wastemaster is that it accepts the waste tank of a Thetford cassette toilet, carried on top. Waste water and toilet waste can thus be disposed of in one journey. A useful item.

> Most of the water that goes into your caravan has to come out again

■ **Above:** *The Wastemaster trolley*

The NEW complete Caravan and Motor Home *Handbook*

Waste containers eventually collect a lining of disgusting grease and general gunge, and need thorough cleaning. Chuck in a handful of sharp sand or gravel, a few pints of really hot water and a squirt of detergent, screw the top on and give it a good shake. After rinsing out use a little disinfectant. This rather dreary chore is rarely volunteered for but is very important. Smelly wastewater containers are a health hazard. Water tank disinfectant and cleaner is available from any dealer's accessory shop.

Plumbing systems

Depending on its age - and we are considering a span of 30 years or more - your caravan will fall into one of four broad categories.

1. **Dead primitive.** *A sink in the kitchen area, a washbasin in the loo, but no taps. You pour your own. Not many still in use today.*
2. **Basic.** *As (1), but a single tap in each location, delivering cold water only, usually via a foot pump sunk into the floor. Again virtually obsolete.*
3. **Comfortable** *(Circa 1980s to mid 1990s.) Hot and cold running water delivered by submersible, self-priming 12-volt electric pump. Water heated by (usually) a Carver gas-fired water heater. This has an underfloor flue and is located in one of the bedding lockers and heats and stores 1 gallon of water - controlled by a thermostat. Later models enlarged to 2 gallons stored.*
4. **Bang up to date - all mod cons.** *Most vans from about 1994 onwards, except those with most basic specifications, have kitchen, washbasin and shower supplied by a dual role gas/mains electric 2- or 3-gallon water heater. Many of these more recent models will have pressurised water systems, whereas group (3) relied on the water pump being activated by the microswitch in whichever tap was turned on. (More on this in a few moments.) Post-1996 up-market vans will also have the Thetford C200 swivel-bowl toilet.*

> Your caravan will fall into one of four plumbing categories

In earlier editions of The Caravanners Handbook we went in detail into the plumbing *(or lack of it)* in groups *(1)* and *(2)*, and how a DIY caravanner could upgrade his plumbing to the next higher level. The time has come, however, to draw a veil over this spartan form of caravanning. There are still some vans about which fall into group *(2)*, and they can be equipped with hot water, but in the new millennium, most caravans will fall into groups *(3)* or *(4)*, so we'll shortly look more closely at these.

There were various stages in between these four groups. Before the days of the Carver stored hot water systems, many vans had a gas-fuelled water heater which heated water, not for storage, but for immediate delivery. It was heated as it passed through the appliance and was delivered via a swivelling long-armed tap. This was much like the old domestic Ascot water heater, and I fitted one to an old 12-foot Astral Ranger caravan. It was considered the very last word in camping comfort. It also eventually scorched the roof.

Back to the present. The majority of caravans today are in group *(3)* and *(4)* and so the water gets into the caravan via the submersible pump. This is fixed at the bottom end of a flexible plastic pipe which has two cores, one for water and one for the wire to power the pump. When this submersible pump was first introduced in the late 1980s, the pump and the pipe rolled up for stowage in a small compartment in the side of the van. The more recent version is detachable, the combined electric and water supply pipe can be disconnected at the point where the water supply enters the side of the van. This is also close to the location of the water heater. Once the Duty Water Person has delivered the full 5-gallon container alongside the van, the pump and hose are lowered into the container. The pump is fully submerged and self-priming.

Main water supply

Forward-looking site operators are steadily introducing 'super pitches' where mains water is supplied directly to the caravan, and waste water similarly disposed of, without any of the fetching and carrying which we all know so well.

Such pitches are equipped with a water supply connection exclusively for your caravan. You will need an adaptor to couple up your caravan to the supply point, after which you have a permanent supply which bypasses your submersible pump. The flow has been suitably reduced in pressure at the supply point in order to avoid damage to your water system.

Water Heaters

A van in group *(2)*, ie with just a cold water supply, could have been equipped with running hot water, delivered to kitchen and washroom using the Carver 'Cascade' gas/mains electric 2-gallon heater which has already been mentioned. The mains electric role employs an immersion heater rated at 660 watts, and the unit can be run using either gas or mains electricity as the power source. For a rapid warm up, both fuel sources can be used at once.

■ *Fresh water connection to caravan*

Now that was the status quo for pre-1997 caravans. Vans built during or after 1997 with Carver water heaters had the new Cascade Rapide heaters.

On the Rapide G/E the electric heating element was upgraded to 830 watts *(well within the scope of most campsite mains hook-ups)*, resulting in a 24% faster heat up to maximum temperature.

■ *Carver Cascade water heater in bed locker*

The gas-only model was redesigned to achieve a faster heating time over the old model.

Following the takeover of Carver Engineering by Truma in 1999, the Carver Cascade gas/electric water heaters were superseded by the Truma Ultrastore heater, which is circular in shape and stores 10 litres of hot water *(2.2 gallons)* against the 2 gallons of the earlier rectangular Carver heater.

Note that, like the Carver heaters, the Truma Ultrastore has a flue or vent on the outside wall of the caravan. The Truma, however, has a plastic cover to the vent which MUST be removed before operating the heater by gas. The current Truma dual-fuel water heater - the B10 boiler has a capacity of either 10 or 14 litres.

See the note on the Truma/Carver takeover at the end of this section.

The majority of caravans equipped with a hot water system currently make use of Carver or Truma equipment, but a number of manufacturers are installing the Belling 'Malaga' heaters. Both companies will gladly supply catalogues and information. 'Malaga' water heaters are marketed by Belling Appliances Ltd. *See Useful Contacts at the back of the book.*

These water heaters are very efficient and safe. Fail-safe technology is employed so that in the event of a fault in the supply of water, electricity or gas, the unit will shut down. They tend to be sensitive to DC voltage drop and need a minimum of 10.5 volts to operate.

Always be on the look out for 'super pitches'

6

The installation of water heaters in an old caravan is within the scope of the competent DIY caravanner. In each case a supply of gas, 12-volt DC current and, for the dual fuel models, mains electric current is needed. As I have stressed elsewhere, if you modify or tap into your gas supply system, do get the system pressure-checked by a caravan dealer's workshop when you have finished. Exactly the same goes for your mains electric installation. Get it checked and a certificate issued.

See the section on *mains electricity.*

If you install or modify a hot water system, do use the correct flexible plastic piping for the job, ie red for hot water, blue for cold. They are designed for the job. Cheap, clear plastic is not. Also, on any modification to your water system, do use jubilee clips. Air gets in and water gets out and that spells trouble.

Always
remember
get the
system
pressure-
checked

At this point it should be noted that flexible plastic piping has been used for caravan water supply systems, however basic, for the past thirty years. That is changing, however, and van manufacturers are now installing water systems using semi-rigid plastic pipes, whose joints are a simple watertight push-fit, so jubilee clips are not needed.

To break into the gas supply you will need a T-joint plus the olives and nuts to make gas-tight compression joints. Also you need a suitable length of copper pipe to feed your new appliance, Make sure you get the correct sized T-joint. You are going to tap into one of the gas supply pipes either underneath or inside your caravan, and the size *(bore)* of these pipes will vary. Consult your caravan dealer for the bits and pieces, they will give you all the guidance you need.

Pressurised Systems

Let us look at more up-to-date water supply systems. We said earlier that the introduction of submersible 12-volt water pumps solved the business of connecting your fresh water container to the caravan. The supply to the van is via a length of twin plastic pipe, one pipe carrying the water and the other housing the 12-volt cable which connects to the submersible pump at the end of the water pipe. This twin pipe, when not in use, rolls up complete with submersible pump and is stored in a small housing in the side of the caravan. We described this accessory earlier, when defining plumbing systems.

This was the standard set-up on group *(3)* vans, but we eased into the group *(4)* era in the mid 90s, when the twin water/electric pipe became a separate item which was plugged into a twin connection on the side of the van. It is at this location that you would stand your fresh water supply in plastic jerrican or Aquaroll. You then simply drop the self-priming submersible electric pump, on its length of twin pipe, into the water container.

Water is then supplied as follows. The submersible pump is connected via the caravan's water inlet point to all the taps in the van. This usually means hot and cold taps at the kitchen sink, the washbasin in the loo, and the shower unit – six taps in all.

Each tap is individually wired to the water pump via a microswitch which, when the tap is turned on, operates the pump and water is delivered to the open tap. In the case of hot water, when the pump operates and builds up pressure in the system, including the cold water feed to the heater, the only exit for the water is through the open hot water tap. So hot water is pushed from the top of the hot water storage tank to the tap by cold water pumped into the bottom of the tank. At this point the water heater thermostat will cause the burner to ignite and heat the newly arrived cold water at the bottom of the heater unit, just like a domestic system.

The main flaw in this set-up is the sometimes unreliable nature of the microswitches in the taps. I have occasionally had to dismantle a tap in order to replace the microswitch and get 12 volt current to the pump. All this prompted the development of a pressurised system which has the advantage of using only one microswitch, and is found in most group *(4)* caravans.

It works like this. The taps have no electric connection with the pump, so when the tap is turned off, the pump goes on pumping, so building up a head of pressure in the system. Very soon a pressure sensitive microswitch senses the appropriate level of pressure and cuts off current to the pump. The pump stops, leaving a degree of pressure in the system. Whenever a

Kitchen sink, washbasin and shower unit? Six taps in all

6

tap is opened again, the pressure in the system causes water to flow, which reduces the pressure. As soon as this drops to a predetermined level, the pressure sensitive microswitch will operate the pump again and the flow of water is maintained.

Nothing is perfect and pressurised systems have two main snags. The first is that if you have even a small leak in the system, the pressure will fall to a level where the sensor causes the pump to start up again, and you wake up in the morning to a kitchen cupboard, or whatever, full of water. It is a sensible precaution therefore to switch off the pump at the caravan's electric control panel at bedtime or when going out for the day.

The second drawback lies with the very sensitive pressure switch which, you remember, gauges the level of pressure in the system and causes the pump to stop or start. This switch works off 12-volt direct current, but unfortunately the actual voltage can vary, depending on your power source. Power from your caravan battery will vary from power obtained from your van's mains transformer. Again, 12-volt power from the transformer, when used on 230 volts in the UK, will vary from the same source when using continental 220-volt mains.

Pressurised
systems are
very good

A small variation in voltage in the 12-volt current will upset the critical setting of the pressure switch, causing too much or too little pressure in the system. So, on the one hand we have microswitches in taps which occasionally prove faulty, and on the other hand, variable voltage can cause a pressure sensitive switch to malfunction, so both systems have their critics. Pressurised systems in the main are very good but totally intolerant of leaks, however small.

The Whale 'Watermaster' system is found in many caravans with pressurised water supply. A comprehensive range of spare parts is available from this very helpful company. **See Munster Simms Engineering Ltd in** Useful Contacts **at the back of the book**. Advice is readily available to any DIY caravanner who wishes to convert his existing water supply to a pressurised system.

My personal advice is: don't bother. If you have a non-pressurised system with microswitches in each tap, then stick to it. Occasionally having to replace a switch is, in my view, preferable to having to adjust the pressure switch to cope with the fluctuations in 12-volt current. If you do have a problem with microswitches playing up, then replace your taps. The 'Whale' range includes some excellent taps, designed for quick and easy replacement of microswitches.

Talking of 'Whale' taps reminds me of a very good accessory for your shower. Showering in a caravan is a bit different. You can't stand there for ten minutes or so with your mind in neutral, enjoying a never-ending supply of hot water like you get at home. You will soon empty your 2- or 3-gallon tank, shortly followed by a hollow gurgling sound from your empty 5-gallon container outside the van.

Hardened campaigners will know that having used your hot and cold taps to get the right temperature, you get in and get good and wet. To save water, you then turn off both taps and give yourself a good soaping.

All right so far? Good. Now the excruciating bit comes when you go to rinse off. When you turn on the taps again, do you get exactly the same temperature as before? Oh dear me, no. It's either blistering hot or icy cold, and in a caravan shower compartment there isn't even room to leap out of the way.

Does all this strike a chord? Take heart, and read on. The 'Whale' wizards have come up with a shower head with a plastic adjustment thingummy which enables you to turn off the water at the shower head – you don't touch the taps. When you are duly soaped you turn on the flow again at the shower head, and normal service is resumed at the same temperature as before. As a service to mankind, I reckon that's worth a Nobel Prize by anyone's standards. This brilliant piece of gismology can be had from most caravan dealers' accessory shops.

Do note, however, that this gadget should only be used where there is a pressure sensitive system. Once the flow of water is shut off at the shower head, the pressure will build up and the pump automatically switches off. That's OK but with microswitches in each tap, if you shut off the water flow at the shower head, as distinct from turning off the taps, the pump will still continue to run, which could damage the system.

As an aid to all-weather caravanning, a well built modern van will have all the water and gas pipes routed through the inside of the van where they are less likely to freeze up in winter weather.

The final word on water supply concerns filters. When 12-volt submersible pumps first appeared in the later 1970s, a screw-in renewable filter was incorporated into Carver systems. This contained carbon granules which filtered out impurities in the water and also helped to remove the taste of chlorine, which was usually present when using water purifying tablets.

Mark III Carver Crystal Plug-in water hose with slim line filter cartridge

6

Hardened
caravaners
know how
to shower

6

This was replaced some 20 years later by the Mark III filter, a neater and more compact job.

Now these filters were fine as long as they were renewed every 30 caravanning days, which of course they weren't. Many owners would settle for replacing the filter during the annual service, which a dealer would automatically do. Sadly, a good number of caravanners would skip an annual service, and forget the water filter. If not replaced regularly, the carbon granules would eventually attract bacteria instead of eliminating them, and the filter is then doing more harm than good.

Around the millennium, therefore, several caravan manufacturers decided that, because of this frequent tendency, and the fact that the past twenty years has seen improvements in the quality of water supplied on sites, particularly on the Continent, they would stop fitting water filters altogether.

So, for the 25 years prior to about 2001, caravans were fitted with water filters and after that, probably no filter at all.

Water quality on sites has improved greatly

If your van has a filter **YOU MUST RENEW IT** at the annual service, or after 30 days use. Failure to do so can involve significant health hazards.

A word of explanation on this water supply section.

We've seen several references to **Carver** equipment; Carver Engineering have been manufacturing caravan equipment for many years -- water supply and heating, caravan space heating, air conditioning and more recently, the Carver electric caravan mover. Much of this equipment is in use bearing the Carver name, but in 1999 they were taken over by **Truma**. Similar accessories are in newer caravans, but branded 'Truma', so from this point on you may find references to either name. Two names but the same company.

The NEW complete **Caravan** and **Motor Home** *Handbook*

Checklist:

Water Supply

1 Use 5-gallon plastic containers, or an 'Aquaroll'. ✓
   Small containers are useless.

2 Buy a small water trolley - it saves a lot of work. ✓

3 Use jubilee clips, fitted tightly, on all flexible ✓
   plastic hose connections.

4 On older vans with manual or foot-operated
   pumps, keep a spare set of washers, diaphragm etc. ✓

5 To install a hot water system use correct high- ✓
   temperature hose (coloured red).

6 Sterilise the whole system annually, ✓
   (See Chapter 12 on the maintenance).

7 On submersible (impeller) pump systems,
   replace the carbon filter annually. This is
   important, since bacteria will grow in the older ✓
   filter cartridge.

8 Remember - drain any water heater before the ✓
   winter lay-up. Frost can cause irreparable damage.

6

Sanitation
Chemical Toilet

About the time of the early '90s, most caravans boasted a built-in 'cassette' toilet. Prior to this, the toilet compartment just had a washbasin and space for a portable chemical toilet.

In the older caravan with no cassette toilet, one had to decide whether or not to carry a portable chemical loo, and this usually depended on whether you would spend all your time on sites with toilet facilities. Caravan Club certificated locations and Camping and Caravanning Club 'hideaways' *(five vans only and usually in a farmer's field)* require you to have your own toilet facilities. However, most, though not all, permanent sites whether club sites or commercial will have at least one toilet block. Even so, do you or your family want to face the task of occasionally trekking, perhaps through the rain, a quarter of a mile or so at 3.00 am?

Assuming you do carry your own toilet, where will you locate it? There are three options: in the toilet compartment in the van or, secondly, in a separate toilet tent *(which is a small tent, like a miniature telephone kiosk, about three feet square)*. A third option would be to have an awning which has a toilet annex – virtually a toilet tent built into the body of the awning.

All chemical toilets are used with a special chemical fluid, which is widely obtainable from accessory shops and often site shops. This is usually a blue-coloured liquid which breaks down and sterilises solid waste matter and also acts as an effective deodorant.

Elsan are among the leaders in the field of chemical toilets and waste treatment, not only for campers but also for sanitation in coaches and aircraft.

They are the producers of a chemical fluid for use in chemical toilets, which is also available in powder form. It is packed in handy sachets which are themselves water soluble and biodegradable, starting to dissolve immediately on contact with water. The sachets are lighter in weight than the equivalent dosage of fluid and consequently easier to store. All chemical toilet preparations are available from most accessory shops.

The toilet unit itself can vary from very simple to quite sophisticated. In its simplest form a chemical toilet consists of a container with a seat and a lid. A step up from this involves an inner bucket or container which can be removed for emptying, and the lid forms a tight seal which keeps the contents where they should be when the caravan is on the move. Ideally, of course, the toilet should be emptied before moving on.

> A trek to the toilet in the rain at 3.00 am?

Two-tank Toilet

Some years ago there was a great step forward with the introduction of two-tank toilets. These consist of a lower storage tank, above which is a conventional toilet bowl surmounted by a seat and a lid. Separating the two compartments is a simple valve which slides sideways to open or close. Around the outside of the upper bowl is a tank containing fresh water with which the bowl can be flushed by using a neat hand pump or, on some models, an electric pump. The whole outfit comes apart, the upper bowl and flushing tank lifting clear of the holding tank. The latter only, with the valve closed, is then taken to the disposal point, and is emptied through a convenient spout which swivels out from the top of the tank. The great advantage of the two-tank variety is the ease of emptying plus the fact that in use the contents of the lower tank remain out of sight.

Two tank toilets are essentially portable affairs

Elsan make a good range of portable two-tank toilets. This is their 'Visa' range in which all models feature twin flushing jets and waste level indicators.

Cassette Toilet

Two-tank loos are essentially portable affairs and can be sited outside the caravan in a toilet tent or wherever. In the late eighties they were eclipsed by a far more sophisticated piece of plumbing in the shape of the 'Thetford' Cassette 'Porta Potti'. A great step forward from portable toilets, the Cassette loo is built into the toilet compartment in the caravan.

The main part of the toilet incorporating the seat, the bowl, flushing-water holding tank and flushing pump is a permanent fixture in the caravan's toilet compartment. The 'cassette' part is the waste-holding tank which slides out sideways from under the assembly through a small trapdoor in the side of the caravan. Even the flushing-water tank is refilled from outside the van. As with some of the portable models there is a waste level indicator to prompt the emptying of the holding tank. The flushing-water tank also has a level gauge. It goes without saying, of course, that the waste tank should only be removed for emptying when the toilet is not in use!

This thought evoked a dim memory from the days when I was soldiering in the Middle East. The loos I remember were a simple corrugated iron structure *(with an inside temperature of about 130°)*. There was a rigid wooden seat, with bucket beneath, which was withdrawn through a trapdoor in the rear of the outfit for disposal. Sadly, the local sanitary operative would frequently whip open the trapdoor and remove the bucket regardless of whether the facilities were actually in use at the time. This could prove inconvenient, to say the least, and at times even painful.

While on the subject of conveniences, I vividly recall a unique piece of war-time military plumbing at a dreadful and primitive camp somewhere in Kent. A communal affair, it consisted of a long piece of 18-inch drainpipe laid along the ground with holes cut along the top at 3-foot intervals, with simple wooden seats attached. Hessian partitions separated one from one's neighbour, but there were no doors so you could sit there and view the rolling Kent countryside in panoramic splendour. This appliance was flushed by discharging a 500-gallon water tank along it at hourly intervals.

There was always a certain level of water in the pipe, however, and much innocent merriment was to be had by loosely bunching up a wad of newspaper, igniting it and floating it along beneath your neighbour, whereupon there would be cries of 'dear oh dear' and 'oh you bounder', and other soldierly expressions.

The principal attraction of this apparatus, however, lay in its flushing mode. When the 500 gallons was on its way, a distant roaring noise could be heard and the more experienced 'campers' would leap clear. Before the wall of water arrived it was preceded by such a draught of wind that, with skilled personnel rising and sitting in concert as it were, the whole thing could be played like a

Toilets have come a long way since a bucket with a seat

vast clarinet. Unfortunately no record of this phenomenon appears in any war diary, which is a pity – it was quite unique.

But I digress. As I said in discussing the excellent Thetford Cassette Porta Potti, just make sure you don't set about emptying it while it is in use. Perhaps some form of whistle signal could be agreed upon.

As with a two-tank toilet, the Thetford Cassette toilet has a waste holding tank which, when not in use, is isolated from the upper part of the appliance by a valve. This is really a plastic shutter which slides horizontally to seal the top of the waste tank. The plastic shutter is bedded up against a circular rubber washer which surrounds the opening to the tank. This provides a watertight seal for carrying the waste tank prior to emptying.

Now, this is a small but important point. The contact between the plastic valve, or shutter, and the rubber washer, must be kept lubricated. Failing this, the sideways movement of the shutter can cause the washer to buckle slightly and the waterproof seal is lost. The top of the shutter and the underside of the washer should be lubricated with a vegetable oil. Olive oil is good, but a mineral oil is likely to perish the washer.

6

Remember to lubricate rubber washers with a vegetable oil **not** mineral oil

Sanitation - Essential Services

Don't overlook this periodic bit of maintenance and when priming the waste tank prior to use, try to pour the chemical toilet fluid cleanly through the aperture into the lower tank. Don't let it dribble down the side of the upper bowl, because it is injurious to this rubber washer. These washers can be replaced but are relatively expensive. The chemical fluid, available in dry powder form in biodegradable sachets, solves this particular problem.

Within a couple of seasons of their introduction, Thetford Cassette toilets were standard equipment in all but the most basic specification caravans, even being shoehorned into small folding vans. They have reigned supreme in the field of caravan plumbing for the best part of 20 years. Now, however, Thetford have gone one better, virtually trumping their own ace with the arrival of the C200.

On this latest model, the upper toilet bowl is oval in shape – viewed from above – and the entire bowl and lid will swivel through 180°. This enables the unit to be sited in a position which takes up the least possible space in the bathroom, but where the user might have insufficient leg room were it not for this facility to rotate the bowl.

The unit must of course be mounted against an outside wall to enable the waste tank to be withdrawn from outside the van. The C200 has a safety device which makes it impossible to flush the toilet when the waste tank has been withdrawn. Flushing is via an electric pump, and the flushing water supply is compatible with onboard fresh water tanks.

The C200 is now standard equipment in most caravans. We've come a long way indeed since the days of the bucket with a seat.

> The C200
> is now
> standard
> equipment
> in most
> caravans

Sanitation

1   Larger and established sites generally have toilets. Certificated locations and Hideaways (often farm locations) do not. ✓

2   Caravan toilets are of three types. The basic ones have a bucket plus a seat. Much better are twin-tank toilets. The most superior type has a seat and flushing-tank permanently built into the caravan, and a cassette-type waste tank which is withdrawn from outside through a trap door. ✓

3   All three need a chemical toilet fluid or powder. ✓

4   Except for the cassette type you keep the toilet either in the caravan loo compartment or a separate toilet tent, or in a toilet compartment built within the awning. ✓

5   There are advantages and disadvantages with all three. ✓

6   After a holiday in the caravan, wash out and disinfect the toilets. Leave valves, filler caps, etc. open to allow air to circulate. ✓

7   Lubricate the valve and washer of a two-tank toilet - including a cassette toilet - with a vegetable oil. ✓

Sanitation - Essential Services

6

Gas Supply

In the absence of mains electricity, cooking and heating depend on gas, as do the fridge and the water heater.

With a modern caravan fridge, there are usually three options: 12-volt electricity, mains electricity or LPG *(gas)*. The 12-volt facility is strictly for use on the move when the moving tow car is supplying the 12-volt current. When stationary, a fridge running on 12-volt current will knock the stuffing out of the car battery in a very short time. When your car towbar and electrics are fitted, make sure your auto-electrician wires the fridge connection so that the car supplies 12-volt current to the fridge only when the car engine is running. A flat battery is the inevitable alternative.

Using mains current for fridge and water heater undoubtedly makes for worthwhile savings in gas. Electric cooking can be considered using a microwave oven.

Back to gas – Liquefied Petroleum Gas *(LPG)*. Butane is more common, but propane may be used. The essential difference is that propane functions at lower temperatures than butane, and is really necessary for mid-winter caravanning when it becomes too cold for butane to flow freely. On the other hand, Butane has a higher calorific valve than Propane, so is more economical.

A regulator must be fitted to the gas cylinder to ensure that, regardless of the volume of fuel in the cylinder, gas is supplied to the appliances at a constant uniform pressure.

The principal fuel sources are either Camping Gaz, Calor gas or Shell. Calor gas and Shell supply propane and butane, Camping Gaz only supply butane and is available throughout many western European countries.

The great majority of British caravanners use Calor gas which is only available in the UK. Calor metal cylinders containing butane are coloured blue and propane cylinders are red.

You should decide on and stick to one brand, since each has its own type of regulator and fittings and they are not interchangeable. However, from Gaslow International an adaptor is available which permits a Calor gas regulator to be used with Camping Gaz if you should run out of Calor gas when abroad.

We have caravanned in France for years, and two of the small-size *(10 lb or 4.5 kg)* Calor gas cylinders have always lasted us through a 16-day holiday, and allowed us to cook and run a gas fridge and a water heater. Today, however, both water heating and fridge can be run on mains electricity -- so gas supplies last even longer.

Larger, 7kg Calor gas containers are available and you should be able to take enough gas abroad with you to cope with anything

> You should decide on, and stick to, one brand of gas

other than an extra long holiday, or a large family. Again, decide which size to go for, since the 4.5-kg size and the 7-kg size have different regulator fittings.

You will have to pay for the hire of your first two cylinders outright; thereafter empty ones are exchanged for full ones, for just the price of the gas. It is usual to carry two cylinders so that you always have a full spare.

Calor gas is easily obtainable throughout the UK at caravan dealers, many garages and hardware shops and, of course at organised campsites. You are not in fact buying the cylinders, only renting them. You should keep your rental receipt in case you wish to hand the cylinders back.

Every year you keep a Calor cylinder, the amount of your returnable hire deposit goes down. At seven years, the refundable amount has dropped to 25%, and it remains at that level for 50 years.

Cylinders are often located in the caravan at the front end, although this varies with the age of the van. On much older vans there were a couple of clamps to locate the containers on the 'A' frame. From here they were fairly easily stolen, or vandals or evil kids could turn off *(or on)* the supply tap as the mood took them.

The next stage was a fibreglass locker located on the 'A' frame which accommodated two gas cylinders plus sometimes a 12-volt battery *(although the battery must now be located in a separate locker from the gas cylinders)*.

Jumbo-size lockers built in to the front end of the body of the caravan soon followed, and these could accept not only gas cylinders and battery, but often a spare wheel and an awning. This solved some major stowage problems but since these were together the four heaviest items to be carried, there was now a weight problem.

The extreme front end of the van is not the best place for all these items unless one keeps careful track of the resultant nose-weight. These gas lockers are capable of being secured *(after a fashion)* with a small lock, and are at least reasonably childproof.

The late 1980s saw the introduction of more aerodynamic caravans with sloping fronts. A large gas locker was built into the front of these, which

> You should always have a full bottle as a spare

stretched across the whole width of the van. Access was via a hinged flap, often supported on gas struts, which lay flush with the front of the van.

This principle of a gas locker contained within the caravan itself is now embodied in a more compact form, with the locker located along the side of the van above the axle, often extending into the wardrobe space. The idea of locating heavy gas cylinders over the axle makes good sense.

Note that LPG is heavier than air and any locker designed for storing gas cylinders will have a ventilator opening on the floor in order to allow any leakage to escape and disperse. These floor vents must NEVER be blocked or covered over.

With the introduction of new safety standards which relate to LPG and electricity, all caravan manufacturers are required, since 1990, to keep the gas cylinders separate from the battery locker and from electric cable runs.

Use the correct type of regulator

When we discussed British and European Standards in Chapter 1, we saw that all 1994 caravans and onwards must be fitted with flame failure safety devices. These prevent the gas ring on the cooker hob being blown out by draught, with gas continuing to escape. It is a most important safety precaution and was long overdue.

The connection between the regulator on the gas cylinder and the caravan's gas supply system is simple. Small bore copper pipe, which feeds the gas appliances in the van, terminates in the gas cylinder storage locker with a brass fitting which accepts a special neoprene tube as a gas tight push-fit, however, a small jubilee clip should always be used as a safety measure. A short length of this tubing goes to the regulator on whichever gas cylinder is in use.

The working pressures of butane and propane differ, so be sure to obtain the appropriate tube. Better still use tubing which covers both butane and propane.

It is also most important to use the correct type of regulator, depending on whether butane or propane is involved, because of this difference in working pressure between the two, butane at 28 millibars and propane at 37.

The neoprene tubing is purpose-made; it is available from caravan dealers, and only this tubing should be used. It does not last forever, and ideally should be replaced every two years. Its cost is negligible. The year of manufacture is printed on it, and should you buy a second-hand caravan with old tubing – replace it. The regulator also will not last forever, and should be replaced after about five years.

The regulator fitting to a Calor gas 7-kg cylinder is a clip-on type, and on the smaller 4.5-kg one it is threaded, so again, different sizes of cylinder require different regulators. Do note

that these 4.5-kg cylinders and regulators have left-hand threads.
Don't waste energy trying to unscrew the regulator from an empty
container when all you are doing is tightening it. Until recently
the butane 4.5 kg cylinders had left-hand threads and the Propane
cylinders had right-hand. Now both butane and propane cylinders
are left-hand threaded.

Gaslow supply a useful gauge to fit between cylinder and
regulator. This will tell you how much gas you have left, and will
also serve to detect a leak in the gas system. You can, however, get
a good idea of the amount of gas left by picking up the cylinder and
comparing it with the other *(full or empty)* cylinder. Since LPG in
the cylinder is in liquid form, sloshing it about will give you a good
idea of the amount contained. A gauge is obviously more accurate.
This gauge is a useful gadget, and is also incorporated into another
really excellent piece of gear.

Sod's Law says that when the gas cylinder runs out, dinner is
about three minutes away from absolute perfection. Not only
does the cooker hob and oven go out, but so do the fridge and the
water heater if running on gas. If the gas cylinders have threaded
connections, the Duty Watch has to find the special spanner,
and go outside to the gas locker and change the connection
from one cylinder to the other, urged on by the cook. The only
torrential downpour of the whole fortnight is timed to coincide
with this event.

The Gaslow Changeover Unit is the answer to all this, it
consists of a gas tube long enough to connect one cylinder to the
other when located in the gas locker. Halfway along this tube is
the regulator, indicator gauge and connection to the van gas supply
system. In use, the outlet valve on one cylinder is switched on and
the other is off. The gauge indicates the level of gas in the cylinder
which is `on'. When this runs out, changing cylinders simply
means closing the valve in the empty cylinder and opening the full
one. Literally a ten-second job and it does stop the catering staff
from throwing a wobbly when a cylinder runs out.

Of course, this doesn't work if both cylinders are empty. In this
case you come in for a lot of verbal from Head Office and another
little chat about forward planning.

For your Gaslow dual connector you will need to get the
right fittings for your cylinders – clip-on connections or threaded
depending on the type of gas cylinders. Gaslow equipment is
stocked by most accessory shops or contact Gaslow International.
See *Useful Contacts* **at the back of the book**. Truma also supply a
simple to operate changeover system between two cylinders which
incorporates a regulator and operates in the same fashion as the
Gaslow. This is the Truma 'Duo-Comfort'. **See** *Useful Contacts* **at
the back of the book**.

Pefect!
A device
to prevent
half cooked
dinners

Now this next item is particularly important, and depends on whether you have a pre-2004 caravan, or one supplied to 2004 specifications and later, because as from September 2003, significant changes in gas supply took place and these are covered by European Standards EN 1949 and EN 12864.

Prior to 2004, caravan gas has been supplied as follows. The gas cylinder *(be it propane or butane)* is secured in its location in the caravan. You then attach an appropriate regulator to the cylinder, whose purpose is to regulate the flow of gas to a pre-determined uniform pressure, regardless of the quantity of gas in the cylinder.

Pre or
Post 2004
caravan?

It makes a
difference

We have seen that propane and butane cylinders require separate regulators, and also different sizes of cylinders take different regulator fittings. After passing through the regulator, gas is fed, now at a much lower pressure, through a flexible neoprene tube to the point where it is joined to the system of copper pipes which feed the various appliances in the caravan. This is usually conveniently located near the bottom of the gas cylinder locker.

However, 2004 vans, and later, have the batting order reversed. Instead of being coupled to the gas cylinder, the regulator is now permanently located in, and secured to, some point in the gas locker, and is connected to the cylinder by a flexible tube which **MUST** now be a high pressure component. The gas then passes through the regulator after which it is fed, at the lower operating pressure, to the van's copper pipe network through the low pressure neoprene tube, as in pre-2004 systems. This connection is best made using a jubilee clip as before.

Three points are worth noting at this stage, two of which will be of some concern to caravan manufacturers.

1. *The days when butane and propane regulators needed different fittings to connect them to a gas cylinder are gone. Likewise, different sized gas cylinders will no longer need separate regulators. This is all due to the fact that the length of high pressure hose which joins cylinder to regulator will have standard brass fittings on both gas cylinders and regulators, using adaptors if necessary. This is a definite plus point.*

2. *Not such a plus point is the fact that this high pressure tube, with its crimped-on end fittings, will be a standard length laid down by EN regulations, and it is pretty short, 45 cms in fact, which is a shade under 18 inches. This will leave the caravan manufacturers very little scope in designing gas cylinder lockers with fitted regulators.*
The high pressure tube will have a warranted life of three years, but located in a gas locker, ie away from sunlight, it should be good for five years. It would be so easy for this to become another 'out of mind' feature, but in the interests of safety, it must be replaced after five years.

3. *The point has already been made that propane and butane operate at different pressures in pre-2004 caravans, butane at 28 millibars and propane at 37 mbs. The new regulators will now deliver both types of gas at a uniform 30 mbs, so van manufacturers will have to ensure that the equipment they install, ie ovens, water heaters, space heaters etc. are plated to confirm that they are designed to operate at 30 mbs.*

For this reason, and others, one should NOT attempt to retro-fit the new regulator system to a pre-2004 caravan.

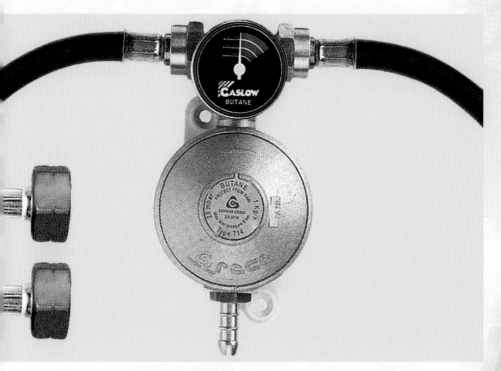

Early in 2003 Gaslow and Grade *(UK)* separated. Gaslow International was formed to deal with all accessories relating to the supply of LPG, and Grade *(UK)* continued to specialise in television antennae for caravans, motorhomes etc.

At this point, Gaslow International expanded their range of products, which now enables caravanners to fit not only the two-cylinder changeover unit described above, but units which give a warning inside the caravan of low gas level. There are also units which warn of gas leaks and even a unit which will automatically change to the full cylinder when the other is empty.

All this equipment is available for both pre and Post-2004 caravans. For post-2004 systems, Gaslow have a unit which enables the caravanner to have both a propane and a butane cylinder in the locker, and to change from one to the other at will.

A very good brochure and price list for their comprehensive range can be had by contacting the company. **See** *Useful Contacts* *at the back of the book*

All the LPG equipment described in this gas chapter, depending on the age of your van, should be available from a well stocked van dealer's accessory shop.

We know that gas powers your cooker, fridge, space heater and water heater *(in the absence of mains electricity)*. Additionally, some older caravans had gas lighting. Many caravanners preferred the homely hissing noise, softer light and warmth of a gas mantle to the harsher light of a fluorescent strip with its frequent radio interference.

The flue of many gas fridges is often vented into the awning, if rigged. For people sleeping in the awning this presents no problem, although there should be some ventilation in the awning.

There is no legal reason why a caravan may not be towed with a gas fridge alight and functioning, although it is not to be recommended. If you really must have your fridge working en route, use the 12-volt electric function of the fridge and run it off your car alternator via the 12S cable. It does consume a lot of current, however, and involves a special wiring job.

What you emphatically must not do is fill up with petrol on your journey while the fridge is functioning on gas. More than one disastrous forecourt explosion has occurred through petrol fumes being ignited by the flame of a gas fridge. This is more likely with a motor home due to the proximity of the fridge air inlet to the petrol pump. Safety regulations forbid any naked flame within 5 metres of a petrol pump.

It is advisable to carry a few spare washers for the connection between the gas container and regulator – the washer here needs replacing fairly frequently. Please note that these washers can be supplied by a caravan dealer's accessory shop. You should **NOT** use the rubber washer which is found inside the black blanking screw cap on a new Calor gas cylinder. The size is identical but the substance of the washer is unsuitable.

If you have gas lighting in the van, carry a spare mantle or two. These should be stored where they will not receive knocks.

A useful tip about gas is, when exchanging an empty cylinder for a full one, try not to be issued with an old or tatty looking cylinder. When containers have been in use for a length of time, a distillation of tarry liquor collects in the bottom of the cylinder. If the cylinder is used until completely empty, this gooey substance can clog your gas appliances or even the regulator. In the case of something like a gas water heater, this can mean an expensive stripping down and cleaning job. Go for a reasonably new looking cylinder, therefore, if you have the chance.

DO NOT fill up with petrol en route if your fridge is gas powered and running

Finally, on the subject of safety, LPG, like North Sea gas, has a strong smelling substance called a stenching agent introduced in order to facilitate a detection of leaks. Escaping Butane or Propane is soon noticed, unless you have a poor sense of smell, which is not uncommon.

For peace of mind you can install an audible electronic gas leak alarm, whose decibels are almost capable of waking the dead. You may remember we said that LPG is heavier than air, so a leak alarm should be installed down at floor level.

And DON'T' block up the floor level ventilators.

In this chapter on LPG in caravans, everything written so far constituted the situation up to February 2006. At this point, however, the picture became a little broader.

At the Boat and Caravan Show at the NEC, a new player in the gas scene appeared, introduced by Truma, who manufacture so many caravan heating appliances.

They announced a joint venture with the petroleum giant BP, who are the largest providers of LPG in the UK. From Spring 2006, Truma are marketing BP GAS LIGHT - a propane gas in a revolutionary new cylinder. Unlike the heavier metal cylinders used by Calor Gas etc., the BP Gas Light cylinder is made from lightweight corrosion proof fibreglass, and weighs about half as much as its steel counterpart when empty. It is claimed to be infinitely safer in that, in a fire, it will slowly melt as opposed to exploding.

Install an audible electronic gas leak alarm

The BP Gas Light cylinders come in two sizes - 5Kg and 10Kg, and are fitted with a 27mm clip on valve which is common to both sizes of cylinder. Additionally, the translucent cylinder allows visual assessment of the volume of gas remaining.

Truma are building a sizeable list of stockists among their existing distributors, and have installed a *BP Gas Light helpline on 01283 586080.* **See photo on page 93.**

A one-off £25 deposit is payable initially on each cylinder, making it simple to swap between 5Kg and 10Kg if you wish. Thereafter, refills cost £12.95 for 5Kg and £16.50 for 10Kg.

Checklist:

Gas Supply

1 Butane (blue cylinders) for everyday use
   Propane (red cylinders) for winter or
   low-temperature caravanning.   ✓

2 On cylinders with threaded outlets, both
   butane (blue) and propane (red) have left-
   handed threads.   ✓

3 Replace the regulator unit after about four
   years. Annually replace the neoprene tube
   which connects the regulator to the caravan
   copper pipe system.   ✓

4 For UK only, Calor gas and Shell supply
   (butane and propane). On the continent,
   Camping Gaz (butane only). You need an
   adaptor to use a Calor gas regulator with a
   Camping Gaz container, from Gaslow
   International or a van dealer.   ✓

5 Have the gas system pressure-checked during
   the annual service.   ✓

6 If you install a gas appliance on a DIY basis,
   have it checked.   ✓

7 Note the differences between pre-2004 and
   post-2004 caravans.   ✓

8 Consider BP Gas Light.   ✓

Electricity Supply (12-volt)

Most of this section applies to caravans as distinct from motor homes.

Before the introduction of 230-volt electricity to touring caravans, the source of electricity was a 12-volt battery. Ideally this was a special `leisure' battery kept in the caravan, or you could plug into the car via the 12S socket and use the car battery. A little further on in this section we explain why a leisure battery in the van is a better option.

European caravans had mains electricity some years before British vans, although on some continental sites the available mains current was as little as 5 amps, and on a few sites this is still the case. We'll come back to mains electricity shortly.

12-volt electric current is still a must in caravans, particularly if you frequent the small get-away-from-it-all sites *(CLs etc)*. Some CLs are equipping pitches with mains hook-ups, but they are still the exception rather than the rule. Internal lights, blown air heating systems, ignition of gas-powered water heaters, flushing of certain marques of cassette toilets, possible portable televisions, built-in car-type radios, the operating of water taps *(via a pump)*, all these home comforts need 12-volt current. In the absence of mains voltage, which will provide 12-volt current via a charger, you need a battery.

In chapter 2 we mentioned that the two 7 pin plugs and sockets *(12N and 12S)* are fast giving way to one 13 pin plug and socket. A European conception, this will soon be standard practice, but for many years to come there will be caravans with the original two 7 pin connections. **See page 105.**

The battery is either in the van, or you use the car battery, or both. One of the connections on the 7-pin 12S socket on the car towbar carries 12-volt power *(suitably fused)* from the car battery and you can plug the caravan lead into the car, when parked close by, to run lights etc.

On the basis that periodic use of the car recharges the car battery, whereas the caravan battery is steadily discharged, it is obviously worth plugging into the car whenever possible and using the caravan battery as a standby when the car is away. You can charge your caravan battery in situ from the car when the outfit is on the move, or charge it in the car boot when the car only is being used. This needs the installation in the car of a special relay, which disconnects the caravan battery when it is not actually being charged and prevents current from the caravan battery feeding back into the car. Charging in the car boot is more effective, since when the battery is in the caravan, the longer wire runs plus plug and socket connections will all cause voltage drop, and a less effective charge is obtained.

6

12-volt electric current is still a must in a caravan

In earlier caravans the battery was often located in the gas cylinder locker, but current regulations have stopped this practice, so if you charge your caravan battery actually in the van, make sure it is in a separate, well ventilated locker, not in the gas cylinder locker. This is because a battery in the process of being charged gives off inflammable gases.

We saw that an amendment to BS 4626 made it mandatory for gas cylinders and 12-volt battery to be stored in separate compartments. EN 1648 – 1 continues this requirement in post-1998 caravans. For some time this was achieved by locating the battery inside bedding lockers, but generating inflammable gases under the bed is not really a good idea, so nowadays caravan batteries are stored in a designated battery locker. These lockers are usually accessed from outside the van and are often located so as to place the weight of the battery as far as possible over the axle. The mains voltage connection point is also located in this locker.

With mains hook ups so abundant we are not often without 230 volts for a long holiday. However, by plugging into the car battery via the 12S connection when convenient, we could easily survive a fortnight without exhausting the caravan battery. We have a 110 amp/hour battery, and with this we run a water pump, an electrically powered caravan mover (of which more later,) a radio/CD player, an electronically governed gas water heater, an electrically flushed toilet and internal lights. *(The small amount of current used to ignite the water heater can be virtually discounted.)* We can be independent of mains electricity if need be.

DO NOT use the thinnest, cheapest wire you can get

We said at the start of this edition that we should occasionally refer to earlier caravans - second or even third or fourth hand, and at this point in chapter 6 we are touching briefly on an era when 12 volt current for an elderly caravan could be drawn from the towcar. This is all irelevant in modern caravans, 99% of which will be wired for mains 230 volts in addition to 12 volt. If mains voltage hookups are available, "nursing" the van's 12 volt battery can be disregarded; it will be constantly kept charged up by the on board charger which is fed by the mains voltage supply.

On a remote site with no mains hookup makes the remarks on 12 volt current much more relevant.

If you wish to install some electrical device such as an extra light or radio/CD player, go to a dealer and tell him what you want to do, and get the correct gauge wire. Don't use the thinnest, cheapest wire you can get, 'because it's only 12-volt'. The resistance offered to a current passing through a wire is in inverse proportion to the thickness. Wire which is too thin will cause undue voltage drop, or even constitute a fire risk if the appliance consumes more current than the wire is designed to carry.

12-volt wiring in caravans varies in thickness – or gauge – between a cross section area of 1 square millimetre $(1 \ mm^2)$ and 2.5 mm². The first will carry a load of about 8 amps and the second a load of over 20 amps. There is a considerable difference therefore, and the gauge of wire you use must be suitable for the current your appliance is going to consume. Do note, however, that these amperage load figures should be reduced by at least 50% once the length of cable involved exceeds 4 metres.

Two points arise here. The first is that caravan dealers' workshops can advise you on any of the above wiring tasks, or better still, carry them out for you. In this case you are secure in the knowledge that the technically correct procedures will be used. The second point is that DIY modifications to your caravan's electric system, mains or 12-volt, will almost certainly nullify a new van manufacturer's existing warranty.

There are, of course, other 12-volt appliances used in caravans in addition to the few we ourselves use. There are vacuum cleaners, fans, electric razors, hair dryers, etc, not to mention television. Fridges, as mentioned earlier, should only be used on 12-volt electricity when on the move, the power being supplied by the car.

Herself has a small hair dryer and a pair of curling tongs, both of which function quite well on 12 volts.

Your choice of battery for the caravan depends on the number of accessories you want to run, and the current they consume. The following is a short list of commonly used 12-volt caravan appliances and a guide to the current they use.

Consider all your appliances before choosing your battery

Appliance	Current (amp)
Single strip light	0.7
Double strip light	1.3
Water pump varies with pump rate of flow	2-4
TV (black and white)	2
TV (colour)	3
Fridge	8

This table shows that a colour TV and a water pump capable of supplying a shower will make a fairly heavy demand on the caravan battery.

A new caravan will obviously be wired correctly and the circuits fused for the equipment that the caravan carries. If you have an older van, however, you may well want to install extra equipment, eg a radio/cassette player or water heater or perhaps a new battery. Any of these tasks would be simplified by asking the Caravan Club to send their excellent leaflet "12-volt Installations in Trailer Caravans." This leaflet covers in detail the choice of battery, the type and size, and also recharging and maintaining it. It gives help with installing and wiring extra appliances and advises on the correct gauge of wire, types of fuses, and so on. The Camping and Caravanning Club can also supply this type of technical advice, and they supply an excellent leaflet on 'Looking after your leisure battery'. Leisure batteries vary from a modest 60 amp/hour to a jumbo size 110 amp/hr. Before opting for the latter, consider the fact that it weights about 60 lb. In basic terms the smaller the battery the sooner it will exhaust itself. Against this, the less current you can consume the longer the battery will last, regardless of its size.

You may go for the option of recharging a small battery whenever you go out in your car, by connecting it up to the relay wired in the car boot. *(Do ensure that the battery is firmly secured.)*

Make sure that the battery in your caravan is a leisure battery as distinct from a car battery.

The essential difference is that a vehicle battery is designed to offer a very heavy load over a short period, as when operating the car starter motor. A leisure battery does just the opposite, it is designed to discharge slowly over a long period while powering, for example, caravan internal lights or starting up a gas powered water heater on a thermostat.

The two types of battery have quite different recharging characteristics, and to use either type in the wrong role over a period of time would be to shorten its life quite considerably.

The 12-volt system in one of our earlier vans had a simple two-way switch on the van's control panel which enabled us to operate

Make sure that the battery in your caravan is a leisure battery

the van lights etc, either from the van battery or the car, having, of course, first plugged into the car with a 12S plug.

This naturally calls for the car to be backed close up to the front of the caravan, which is not always convenient. I therefore had an extension cable about 3 or 4 metres long. This was twin core cable connected to the live accessory pin and the negative, or 'return' pin in the 12S plug and socket at each end of the extension cable. Keep such an extension cable down to a reasonable length, however, because of the possibility of voltage drop. This is a useful accessory if you often use small sites with no mains hook-ups.

In addition to your in-van electrical gadgets you have the road running lights, side, tail, stop, number plate, indicators and – where fitted – high intensity rear fog-light plus the 'outline marker' lights. All these functions plus your domestic lights and appliances are powered from the car, when car and caravan are connected via the two 7-core umbilical cables and 7-pin plugs, and sockets.

The caravan half of these 7-core cables usually terminates inside one of the bed lockers, and there you will probably find your fuses. On later caravans, the fuses may well be near the caravan's electrical control panel. Make sure you know where to find and identify them, and be sure to carry some spares.

The two 7-pin sockets are attached to the car, close to the towball, the two plugs are on cables attached to the caravan. The 12N *(N for Normal)* plug and socket are coloured black, and carry all the connections for the caravan's road running lights, as listed above.

The 12S *(S for Supplementary)* plug and socket are coloured grey or white, and they cater for internal caravan functions. The connections between plugs and sockets are via pins and tubes *(male and female)* and you will be glad to know that it is impossible to connect the 12N plug to the 12S socket or vice versa.

At this point we must introduce a slight complication. In Chapter 2 *(Towbars)* we said that August 1st 1998 saw a European ruling calling for all `S' registered cars to be fitted only with towbars which were EU approved. Something else happened in 1998, this time to do with the wiring of 12S plugs and sockets.

A new European Standard came into force on September 1st 1998, which amended the previously established roles of the 7 pins and tubes in the 12S plugs on caravans. This established a separate earth return pin for fridges operated on the move. In addition, the pin previously used for charging the caravan battery in transit was taken out of use, and battery charging was re-allocated to another pin.

A note that if your car had previously towed an older caravan and you subsequently bought a post September 1998 caravan, the

Familiarise yourself with your caravan's fuse control panel

wiring to your car 12 S socket would need to be modified, in order to be compatible with the new 12S plug wiring, otherwise the fridge would not function on the move nor would you be able to charge your caravan battery.

Around 2008/2009 the two 7 pin 12 volt plugs and sockets began to be superseded by 13 pin assemblies with, of course, 13 core cables, which combined to assume the duties of the older two 7 pin items.

This arrangement originated on the continent and has gained a rapid foothold among British manufacturers. What, you might say, happens to your 12 volt functions when you acquire a new caravan with a single thirteen pin plug and you wish to tow it with your existing car which has the conventional two seven pin sockets on the towbar? A good point, with a simple solution. You have to purchase a modification in the form of a short piece of cable which is so wired to have 12n and 12s plugs merged into a 13 pin socket. In due course all caravans and all tow cars will be wired with 13 pin connections. Bailey, for example, already use 13 pin across their whole range of vans.

The plugs and sockets are not indestructible. Damp gets in inevitably and corrosion sets in, grub screws seize up and so on. They are not difficult to replace. New ones of both types are available from caravan dealers and motor accessory shops. With a new plug and socket you will get a wiring diagram; all the pins are numbered and all the wires are clearly colour coded.

Many failures of internal or road lights are due to faulty connections via corroded plugs, or bad earth connections on side lights, indicators and so on. They are simple to check and correct.

Mains Electricity (220/230 volts)

Coming to the subject of mains *(220/230-volt)* electricity makes me stop and reflect a little. The earliest caravans were horse-drawn, illuminated by an oil lamp, and cooking was done over a wood fire by the roadside. We have progressed a long way since then, and I wonder where it will stop. My family have caravanned for nearly 40 years and we love it, with its implications of a slightly more basic way of life. We are all for lightweight chassis, insulated bodies, double glazed windows and yes, hot running water, but if we insisted on absolutely every modern convenience I think we would prefer to stay in an hotel. We always said we could manage very well without television for starters. A fortnight free of the haunted fish tank had to be a blessed relief, and so far we're still holding out.

We held out for some time against mains electricity, but kicking and screaming, we were swept along with the onward march of progress, and now of course, we wouldn't be without our mains hook-up. I think it would be almost impossible now to buy a new caravan or even a trailer tent which was not wired up for mains power.

One of our earlier caravans did not have mains electricity and rather than having it installed we invested in a transformer called a 'Ranger Power Pack'. It converted on-site mains current - English and continental - into 12-volt direct current. We just plugged our caravan 12S plug into the compact 'Ranger' unit, instead of plugging into the car. *(The unit had both 12S and 12N sockets.)*

The transformer sat underneath the caravan, plugged into the site hook-up point, and gave us a constant 12-volt supply, as well as keeping the caravan battery constantly charged up. In fact with a 'Ranger' unit, one would not need to carry a caravan battery if always camping on sites with mains hook-ups. It is an ideal accessory for an older caravan not equipped for mains power.

Electricity? A good friend but an awful enemy

Our present caravan is obviously mains equipped and on sites with hook-ups we use an electric kettle and toaster and also run the fridge on mains. Both these functions represent a significant saving of gas. In addition the on-board mains powered battery charger gives us unlimited 12-volt current. Water pump for taps and shower, radio/CD and lights can be used without concern for 'nursing' the caravan battery. Both our water heater and our space heater can be powered by either gas or mains electricity, so with a mains hook-up this represents another saving on gas.

We do use sites without mains electricity however. Summer holidays are usually spent on the continent where there are indeed mains hook-ups on most sites, but short breaks often find us in the corner of a remote field in Derbyshire or the Yorkshire Dales, with only basic facilities. Having said that, I notice that an increasing number of Certificated Locations and similar sites are now being equipped with mains hook-up points.

You do of course still have a comprehensive 12-volt system for lighting, water pump, the gas powered water heater, radio and so on. The mains circuit usually gives you two or three conventional flat 3-pin sockets for mains appliances, plus the invaluable facility for keeping the caravan battery fully charged.

The 230-volt appliances used must be carefully considered for consumption, since on most UK sites with mains hook-ups, the maximum current you may consume at one time is from 10 – 6 amp. On non-club and continental sites it can be much less. If the wattage supplied is exceeded, a circuit breaker operates and you and your neighbours are without power.

Don't take the 3 kW kettle from home. A mains kettle used in a caravan should not be of a higher rating than 1000 watts. It would consume about 4 amps and that might well prove to be about enough on some sites.

With grateful acknowledgements to the Camping and Caravanning Club, and in particular to their technical officer, I can do no better than quote certain extracts from a Club's guidance leaflet on mains electricity for campers and caravanners, as follows:

"The Club will allow any kind of camping outfit - caravan, trailer tent, motor caravan or tent - to connect to electric hook ups on Club sites. The Club will be responsible for the safety of the electrical system up to the outlet socket on the hook up post. It is the responsibility of the camper to ensure that the mains electrical cable from the hook up point to the unit and the unit's installation are safe.

Electricity is a very good friend but an even worse enemy. Remember that when camping on a site, the provision of electricity is for temporary use and requires even more care than in the home.

Hook up posts. Each Club hook up post is individually protected against overload by a Miniature Circuit Breaker (MCB) and a Residual Current Device. The MCB is a safety measure and limits the amount of current you can draw from the mains. Most hook ups on Club sites have a maximum rating of 10 amps, although some have 16 amps.

To avoid accidental operation of the circuit breaker and consequent loss of supply, make sure that the total wattage of the equipment you have switched on at any one time is less than 2400 watts or 3800 watts for 16 amp sites.

The following chart shows how many watts or amps normal appliances may use. It is only a guide and power ratings do vary. Add up the wattage or amps for each of your own appliances in use at any one time. The total should not exceed 2400 watts or 10 amps. If you are hooked up to a 16 amp connection the wattage can rise to 3800.

Appliance	Watts	Amps
Domestic Kettle	2000	8.3
Camping kettle	750	3.1
Domestic fanheater	1000	4.2
Camping fanheater	750	3.1
Refrigerator	125	0.5
Toaster	1300	5.4
Iron	1300	5.4
Microwave	1200	5.0
Water heater	660	2.75
TV black and white	30	0.1
TV colour	90	0.4
Battery charger	100	0.4
Hair dryer	600	2.6

These are only average figures. More accurate power figures for wattage or amperage are marked on the appliance itself.

Please note that microwaves are often described as `600 watt'. This is the power they require to run – starting power can be as much as twice the stated wattage."

Thanks to the Camping and Caravanning Club for this useful extract.

> At this point it might be useful to repeat a formula which was dinned into me during Physics at school: –
>
> Volts = Watts ÷ Amps
>
> Amps = Watts ÷ Volts
>
> Watts = Volts x Amps
>
> which should help you with your sums.

To put these three terms into perspective, watts refers to the consumption of current by an appliance whereas volts and amps refer to the supply of current.

A heater or a kettle would be rated in watts, eg 1000 watts, or 1 kilowatt, this being the amount of current the appliance consumes.

The supply of current, eg 230 volts, can best be described as the pressure at which it is supplied, as in the pressure at which hydraulic fluid is forced along a pipe.

Amps refers to the quantity of current supplied or available, eg 16 amps could be the available total amperage supplied at a hook-up point on a camp site.

Mains electricity is not without its hazards

Note that both volts and amps can decrease if either inadequate size of cable or excessive distance *(cable run)* is involved.

Mains electricity in a caravan is not without its hazards. Incorrectly used or installed it can be lethal. British wiring regulations imposed on installations and the supply of current tend to be more exacting than their continental counterparts. For example, electricity supplied on British hook-up points has known polarity, that is, live current is supplied through the positive wire and returns through the negative or neutral wire. For this reason British switches – which turn the appliance on and off – are single pole, which means that only the live wire is cut when switched off.

It is possible to hook up to some continental points and get the polarity reversed. This is particularly common on some French camp sites. What in fact is happening with reversed polarity is that live or positive current is supplied through the negative or neutral wire, and is returned through the positive wire. In other words the current is flowing the wrong way round.

My first memorable experience of the French domestic electricity supply goes back over 40 years, when we used to stay in a delightful, homely, slightly primitive family hotel in Brittany.

There was one toilet per floor and it was lit by a 40-watt bulb. Some energy conscious character had cunningly wired this so

Avoid feeding current through a door bolt

that the brass bolt which locked the door completed the circuit and switched on the light. This ensured that it was impossible to leave the light on when leaving.

■ W4 mains tester unit.

As French toilets go it wasn't bad, though no doubt it has now been modernised. It's probably got a 60-watt bulb and a low level cistern with one of those magic buttons which you lift in order to flush. Back in the late fifties however it still had the original cast-iron, high-level cistern. This was supported on ornate wrought-iron brackets, and along the front, cast in relief, was the name of the originator, one Hercule Leclerc *(1929)*.

For flushing purposes good old Hercule had supplied a generous length of elegant metal chain, and having completed the flushing process one day, I released the brass bolt on the door while still holding on to the chain. I promptly got 220 volts up one arm and down the other.

Why operate the bolt while holding the chain? You may well ask. I don't know, I just did. I can tell you that you only do it once, it does tend to make the eyes water.

Feeding current through a door bolt is bad enough; on top of this the circuit was doubtless earthed through the domestic water pipes, hence the current going to earth via the toilet chain and me.

Confused by reverse polarity? Ask for info from one of the clubs

■ Short Crossover cable for reversed polarity.

6

We love France and the French people dearly; they have contributed much to civilised society as we know it, but domestic electrics is not one of their stronger points.

It has been hinted that I seem to know more about eccentric sanitary facilities than caravanning, and that I would be better employed writing a book about mcmorablc privvics. Maybc I will. For now, however, back to mains electricity.

We were discussing reversed polarity, where the current is incorrectly flowing into the appliance via the return wire, and returning via what should be the positive, or live wire. Using a British single-pole switch under these circumstances means only cutting one wire, but with reversed polarity we would be cutting what is in effect the neutral wire. This means that live current is still flowing into the appliance, even though the switch is 'off', because the current is flowing and returning through the wrong wires.

If caravanning abroad, it is strongly recommended that you purchase, from an accessory shop, a simple and inexpensive gadget called a W4 mains tester. This plugs into one of your standard flat 3-pin mains sockets, and by means of three small neon lights it will warn you if you have reversed polarity, and most importantly it will warn you if you have no earth. I have on several occasions detected reversed polarity on continental sites, and corrected the situation very simply, as follows.

To cope with reversed polarity you need two or three feet of three-core cable, the same gauge as the mains cable leading from the caravan to the hook-up bollard. You also need an extra plug and socket for mains cables. These are both coloured blue and conform to what used to be BS 4343, but is now BS EN 60309 – 2. On the other hand, you could chop off a couple of feet from your existing mains cable. Do this at the caravan end, the end which has the female socket attached

Replace this socket on the mains cable with your new socket, taking care that the three wires in the cable are fitted to the correct terminals on the socket.

Your mains cable is now back as it was before, only a little shorter. You also have a two-foot length of cable with a female socket on the end. You must now connect the new male plug to the other end of the short piece of wire, but connect the live and neutral wires to the wrong terminals. In other words, **change the live and neutral wires over with each other so that the brown (positive) wire goes to the – terminal and the blue (negative) wire goes to the + terminal. The earth wire (yellow/green) must of course always be connected to the earth terminal only.**

If on hooking up to the camp site mains you find, via the W4 tester plug, that reversed polarity exists, disconnect the mains cable from the hook-up bollard, then disconnect the mains cable from the caravan. You now insert your two-foot length of 'changeover' cable between the caravan and the mains cable, and reconnect the mains cable to the camp supply point. The camp supply has reversed polarity, but by interposing your 'crossover' length of wire, the current enters the caravan correctly wired.

This 'crossover' piece of wire and the W4 mains tester was referred to in a really first class article on mains electricity which appeared in the Camping and Caravanning Club's magazine during the summer of 1992. It was written by the late Ralph Lee, the Club's very knowledgeable *(dare I say veteran?)* technical officer. At that time the article unveiled many of the mysteries of electrical lore in very easy to understand terms. I am indeed grateful to Ralph and to Peter Frost, the magazine's *(then)* editor for allowing me to paraphrase some of this most informative feature.

The article likened the flow of electricity through wires to the flow of water through hose pipes. Imagine an electric cable attached to a simple apparatus, such as a light bulb. The current flows through the live or positive wire, heats up the filament in the light bulb and returns through the neutral wire.

> Fires have been started by coiled-up live wires

Ralph drew a parallel between this and a simple water turbine driven by water pumped through a 'supply' hose pipe. The water drives the turbine, then returns to the reservoir through a 'return' pipe. If however, water were flowing to the turbine through the return pipe and returning via the supply pipe, you would, in electrical terms, have reversed polarity.

We can carry this analogy a stage further, and consider an electrical 'residual current device'. Suppose there were a leak in one of the hose pipes carrying water to or from our turbine, then water would be returning to the reservoir at a lower rate than that at which it was pumped out. If we had meters to detect the imbalance between the two rates of flow, we could then shut down the pump and prevent further leaks.

That is exactly what a residual current device *(RCD)* does in an electrical installation. If current is leaking from the circuit and going anywhere other than where it is intended, then an RCD will cut off the current in milliseconds.

Caravans fitted for mains electricity are fitted with RCDs and with fuses, or 'trips' which also break the circuit in the event of an overload of current, or a short circuit.

We spoke of a mains cable to enable you to connect your caravan with the nearest hook-up bollard on the camp-site. This should be obtained from your caravan dealer and will be supplied in the correct gauge wire, which means that each of the three core wires must be 2.5 mm2. The cable should be a minimum of 25 metres in length, and it will be fitted with BS EN 60309-2 blue plug and socket.

The humble but essential mains hook up cable is one of the most abused pieces of caravanning equipment.

DO NOT install or modify mains electricity unless qualified

Walk round any site and you will see what I mean. When vans are sited close to a hook-up bollard, not all the 25 metres of cable is needed, so what happens to the spare? It is, in most cases, either left tightly wound on its carrying drum, or worse, it is dumped under the van all ravelled up like some tangled piece of knitting *(see the photo below)*.

One version looks neat, the other looks tatty, but **BOTH ARE DANGEROUS.**

Wire which has a current passing through it, and is either coiled up or tangled up, actually generates a magnetic field, PLUS heat. I am advised by a Fire Brigade officer that quite serious fires have been started by coiled-up live wires.

If your hook-up cable is too long, get rid of the spare by laying it out as illustrated on next page.

I have gone one better. Having found myself frequently close to the hook-up point, I've bought a spare cable from a motorhome dealer which is only about 10 metres long. I carry both with me and use whichever is appropriate for the site.

I cannot over-emphasise the fact that installing or modifying mains electricity in a caravan should not be tackled by an amateur, no matter how good his DIY achievements. If your caravan is not equipped for mains electricity and you wish to have it installed, then have it done by a qualified electrician who is authorised by the NICEIC *(the National Inspection Council for Electrical Installation Contracting)*.

Lay up extra long mains hookup cable like this to prevent build up of heat

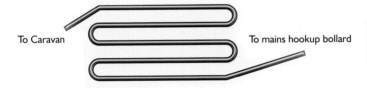

To Caravan   To mains hookup bollard

There are people who advertise in caravan magazines who will come to your location and wire up your van for mains electrics, and many are genuine, capable people. If you want to go down this road, however, take heed of the following.

a.   **There are cowboys in this field, as in many others.**

b.   **The price you pay usually reflects the quality of the job - there are no real 'bargains'.**

c.   **Ask the bloke if he is accredited to the NICEIC. If he's not, don't touch him.**

d.   **When the job is done, you should get a certificate of installation, identifying the contractor as a member of NICEIC.**

e.   **Remember it is your life and the lives of your family which are at risk if you cut corners. Get it done by someone who knows what they are about.**

Any new or second-hand caravan with mains power should be sold with an electrical inspection certificate, and any mains installation should be inspected annually for the sake of your own safety and that of your family.

Spare fuses should always be carried, and it is also a good idea to keep one each of the road light bulbs as spares. It is worth noting that in France it is mandatory to carry spare road light bulbs for both car and caravan.

This is a complicated subject and I have only touched on it here. If you are going to invest in a van with mains electricity, or have it installed in an existing van, do read up the subject first. Ask the Caravan Club for their excellent explanatory leaflet called Hooking up to Mains, or ask for advice from the technical officer of the Camping and Caravanning Club.

The National Caravan Council publish A Guide to Electrical Installations in Touring Caravans. They eventually decided to withdraw this from general circulation, and make it available only to the trade, not the general public. Behind this move lies the conviction that installing mains electricity in a caravan is not a DIY job, and I would wholeheartedly endorse this view.

There are currently a number of accessory firms who advertise kits for installing mains electricity in vans, but as safety standards become ever more strict, these people may well find themselves having to withdraw this gear from sale. Repeat. Installing mains electricity is a job for a professional, and a qualified professional at that.

We ourselves used to think that mains electricity and touring caravans don't go together – we didn't like to think of all that rain water and all that electricity. Progress has overtaken us, however, and mains electricity is now the rule rather than the exception. Certainly, if properly installed and properly serviced it is very safe and a great convenience. Probably we're just old-fashioned. Horse-drawn caravanners at heart.

Electrics

1 On 7-pin or 13-pin plugs and sockets joining car and caravan, keep all connections clean and free from corrosion. ✓

2 Keep all earth connections on the caravan body/ chassis clean (commonest cause of malfunction of road lights). ✓

3 Use a proper leisure battery, ie a boat and caravan battery in your van, not a car battery. ✓

4 Don't run your fridge off a 12-volt supply unless actually towing (on the move) - you'll flatten your car battery. ✓

5 Locate and familiarise yourself with the caravan fuse panel. ✓

6 Keep a few apropriate spare fuses handy in the caravan. ✓

7 To install mains electricity in a caravan go to a member of NICEIC. Don't do it yourself. ✓

8 Use correct low-consumption mains appliances, or you will blow the camp-site circuit. ✓

9 Check the power available. Continental sites generally supply power at a lower amperage than the UK sites. ✓

10 If you're not familiar with 'RCD' and 'reverse polarity' (and who is?) do request information from one of the clubs. They will gladly send you a simple but comprehensive leaflet on mains electricity. ✓

11 Caravan mains are a litte more involved than domestic mains. Don't take chances that would put the lives of your family at risk. ✓

12 A useful formula to remember: Watts = Volts x amps ✓

Caravan Heating

6

Unless you are a strictly Mediterranean/fair weather only sort of caravanner, some kind of heating is essential. Even English summer evenings can be chilly. You can always warm up the van a little by lighting a couple of burners on the cooking hob, but this is scarcely efficient or economical and is potentially dangerous.

Gas was the earlier source of heating power, used in some sort of space heater. Heaters are not found as standard equipment in older caravans and **we made reference in** *Chapter 1*, when discussing internal fittings, to the fact that older vans may have had a gas heater fitted, but with no external flue. These are indeed quite safe provided that adequate ventilation exists.

Comfort in a caravan goes hand-in-hand with technology

Modern caravans are all equipped with some form of heating, usually a gas fired or gas/electric space heater fitted with an external flue. The smaller heaters are flued or vented through the caravan floor; larger capacity heaters have a small stove pipe, or chimney, which emerges through the roof.

There are a number of efficient systems made, but probably the one most commonly fitted as original equipment is that produced for many years by Carver and later developed by Truma *(UK)*.

Obviously caravan sizes vary considerably and so too must a suitable heater. Carver had for some years made three sizes of gas fired heaters: the 1800, 2000 and 3000. The output from these has varied from the equivalent of 1.6 kW to an impressive 3.2 kW, with gas consumption varying proportionately. 1997 saw the range overhauled and the ignition system greatly improved.

From this point onward the range included the 1800 SC, suitable for vans for up to about 16 feet, and the 3600 STC Auto for vans up to 21 feet. The 1800 SC *(and SC Auto)* were vented and flued under the caravan floor, and were available with either piezo spark or 12-volt automatic ignition. The 3600 STC Auto was roof flued and fitted with a 12-volt automatic ignition system. All three featured a flame failure safety device whereby, in the event of the flame being extinguished, the gas supply is automatically cut off.

Following the rapid expansion in the availability of mains electric hook-ups on caravan sites, accessory manufacturers lost no time in converting our previously gas-powered comforts and goodies into electric ones. The mid '90s saw the introduction of the Carver 'Fanmaster' heater, which used mains voltage as the power source to heat air which is then distributed by a 12-volt fan around the caravan. On sites with no mains hook-up availability, the 'Fanmaster' can be used in the normal gas-powered mode. Note that the two fuel options should never be used simultaneously. Many of these dual-fuel heaters are still in current use.

1999 caravans saw the dual fuel principle continued with the Carver range updated to offer mainly the 2000 and the 4000 Fanmaster series.

1999 also saw the German firm Truma acquire the gas heating part of Carver & Co, and caravan heating appliances can currently be found under both the Carver and Truma brand names, and since this book deals with caravans of widely differing ages, you will find both names occur in the text.

Truma *(UK)* Ltd. to give them their full title, progressively acquired the entire business of Carver & Co *(Engineers)* Ltd., and took over where Carver left off in continuing to develop caravan equipment in the fields of heating, water, gas and electricity supply, and of course, the innovative 12-volt caravan mover.

Widely used on modern caravans is the Trumatic range of caravan heaters, some available in modified form for use in motor homes.

Briefly, the range consists of three sizes of gas heater plus the Ultraheat duel fuel heater. The Trumatic S2200 has a heating capacity of 1850 Watts, the S3002 of 3400 Watts and the S5002 of 5500 Watts. The Ultraheat has three power levels, 500, 1000 and 2000 watts, adjustable to suit the camp site's supply. It can be powered by gas or electricity, or both together.

The Trumatic gas heaters can be supplemented by fans and ducting to distribute warm air throughout the caravan, along the same lines employed by the earlier Carver blown hot air systems.

Heating equipment does not stop there, and Truma have a comprehensive and well illustrated brochure which fully describes all the heating and air conditioning equipment available, plus the electric Mover, for both single and twin axle caravans, the successor to the Carver Caravan Mover. **See** *Useful Contacts* **at the back of the book.**

> Some kind of heating is essential

We have made the point elsewhere that increased comfort in caravan goes hand in hand with advanced technology, and the equipment designed for modern water, gas, electricity, refrigeration and air conditioning services is necessarily getting more and more complicated. You can't be expected to take it all in at once, so DO use the manufacturer's handbook; DO sit through the video several times *(if one is supplied)*; DO pay heed to the dealer's advice during the handover of your new *(or second-hand)* caravan; DON'T hesitate to ask him to go over it again if you are not sure. HE IS THERE TO HELP.

Onboard
Equipment and Accessories

General Needs

Even the most luxurious caravan will not offer total comfort by itself and so in your 'payload' you must include basic items such as gas cylinders, a battery, water containers *(unless the van boasts a built-in water tank as most motor homes do)*, the essential spare wheel, jack, step, chocks, some form of spirit level, plus cooking pots and pans, crockery, cutlery, glasses, tin opener, corkscrews, bedding, pillows, tea towels and washing-up gear, towels for the beach and bathroom, toilet kit, personal clothing including macs and wellies, books, games, children's toys, a torch, folding chairs, sunbeds and so on. Last but not least include a first-aid kit, sewing kit, tool kit and fire-fighting equipment.

Some of these items need no comment; some are worth a few words. They all contribute to total weight, and we will consider shortly just how much they add up to. Do save weight where possible - small savings here and there add up to quite a lot when considering the total.

> Crockery should preferably be made of lightweight melamine

Kitchen Gear

An excellent set of nesting aluminium pans with removable handles is available. They have a non-stick finish *(which on ours has now nearly disappeared but we have had them for many years and they have more than paid for themselves)*. When stacked they take up very little room and weight is minimal. We have a kettle and teapot made of aluminium, again of minimal weight. If we know we shall have a mains electricity hook-up, we take an electric kettle and toaster. Crockery should be preferably be of lightweight melamine, available from accessory shops - lightweight, colourful and easy to clean, they are virtually unbreakable. Drinking glasses also are available in clear plastic, in a variety of shapes and again light and unbreakable.

Bedding

This is a matter of choice and expediency. Particularly for children, sleeping bags are the obvious answer, lightweight, easy to make up and stow away. Two sleeping bags can be zipped together to make a double, but sleeping bags don't suit everyone. Sleeping bags should not be too heavy. If you have a 21st century van with a fixed double bed, then of course similar bedding to home is the answer, be it sheets and blankets, or duvet.

Clothing

Items of personal clothing should be kept to a minimum – it adds up in terms of weight and volume at an alarming rate. You obviously don't need much in the way of guernseys and thermal underwear if you're making for the Mediterranean in August, but nearer home some warm clothing should be taken. There is nothing more miserable than being cold.

If you are going to an established site in the summer, there are usually laundry rooms. We are not really into heavy laundry sessions when on holiday, but rinsing out lightweight shirts, tops and underwear is a simple enough matter in the caravan.

You can usually rig up a short clothes line, or you can buy a folding rack which clips on to an open caravan window ledge and is ideal for drying 'smalls', tea towels, etc. outside. I can promise you that you won't wear half the clothes you take with you, so keep the wardrobe list short.

First Aid

A first aid kit is essential

A good medical/first aid kit is essential. You can make up one for yourself with a little thought. We carry ours clearly marked in a plastic ice-cream container, with lid. Apart from the obvious first-aid items, carry some disinfectant, remedies for upset stomachs, and some insect repellent plus sting relief cream for insect bites. A chemist will gladly advise you on what to include.

If going abroad, some water purifying tablets are worth using. They are available from accessory shops and are a wise precaution against the questionable drinking water found on some sites.

Fire-fighting Equipment

A fire extinguisher is something I hope you will never need, but if you do need it then you need it urgently! Would you really take that chance just to save a few pounds? *(£s or lbs.)* You need the dry powder type of extinguisher which is usually available in the minimum recommended 1 kg size; it comes with a quick-release mounting bracket and should be sited near the exit door. With constant towing the dry powder in the extinguisher can settle and become compacted. Take it out of its holding bracket occasionally, invert it and tap it a few times to keep the contents loose.

We also carry a fire blanket which - unlike an extinguisher - lasts forever *(if unused!)*. This is usually kept near the kitchen in case of a cooking pan fire. It really is better to be safe than sorry.

On the subject of fire, all new vans sold after 1 March 1990, and indeed a number sold before then, will have upholstery containing Combustion Modified High Resilience foam *(CMHR)*, to avoid the dense toxic smoke given off by the older stuff. Additionally, from April 1991, the actual furnishing fabrics will be fire-resistant.

For older caravans with pre-fire-resistant upholstery, a very useful flame-resistant spray is available from the Humbrol paint people. Spray it on furnishing fabrics, curtains, etc. Long lasting and non-staining, it is available from DIY stores.

Smoke Alarms

It is a condition of membership of the National Caravan Council that caravan dealers must fit a smoke alarm, if not already fitted, to all second-hand caravans which pass through their hands.

These smoke detectors will differ from the ordinary domestic version, in that there will be a facility for switching them to a lower key or less sensitive mode for a short period of a few minutes, while the caravanner takes a shower, cooks toast or bacon or whatever, since these activities within the confines of a caravan would trigger off a normal domestic smoke alarm.

This modification is important, since one must avoid a situation where you become irritated by false alarms to the point where batteries are removed, or the detector is taken down and stuffed out of sight in a bedding locker. A smoke alarm installed in a caravan should comply with **BS 5446 Part 1.**

Caravan dealers MUST fit a smoke alarm

Smoke produced by culinary activity reminds me of a bloke who would tell all and sundry that his wife was a cordon noir cook. 'You knew exactly where you stood', he used to say. 'If you couldn't smell burning, it was salad'.

Manual Caravan Manoeuvring

Like many of our treasured little luxuries the concept of the electric powered caravan mover is not new.

Carver were, I believe, the first to introduce a workable version and, following the takover, Truma have continued its development and there are now several makes available.

Prices vary but the principle involved is common to all, ie driving the caravan wheels with an electrically driven small wheel which is located firmly up against the van wheel. The small driving wheel has a rough surface, to obviate any slipping between the surfaces of the driven and the undriven wheel. Steering is achieved like any tracked vehicle by applying the motive power to one or other of the caravan wheels. Forward, reverse, left turn, right turn are all achieved by varying the power applied using a handset with buttons, like the remote control of a TV set.

Drive units can be fixed by the average DIY person

Originally the instructions were conveyed to the drive units on the caravan via a multi-cored cable, but eventually this was superseded by a completely remote unit using radio waves.

When not in use, our Bailey Ranger two berth lives behind the house alongside my garage, out of sight of the road. Getting it there involved pushing it up a slight incline, a process which, for many years, Herself and I have achieved without much effort, but the combined effects of arthritis, angina and anno domini have caused us to think again.

We chose a Powrwheel mover which was rapidly and efficiently installed one morning by their local fitter.

■ Mr. Shifta Mk. 3

The two driving motors were fixed just ahead of the two van wheels. The unit's small roller wheels are engaged onto the van wheels by means of a cam which uses a strong spring to locate the unit up against the van wheel. The photo shows this with the reversible socket and wrench used in activating the small driving wheel, much like a torque wrench.

■ *The Powrwheel control unit is located near the battery box in a bed locker.*

So far, so good. Now Powrwheel, who are based in Christchurch near Bournemouth, have brought out a new version of the above, called 'Innovation' which is absolutely brilliant. The lever for locating the small roller against the caravan wheel has gone and the multi-function handset has been redesigned and now the driving rollers can be positioned by a press of a button on the handset. Doing this manually with the long wrench thing was not actually lfie threatening, but for the elderley, the handset versus the torque wrench is simply no contest.

The newly designed driving unit is now totally enclosed, using technology favoured for formula one racing cars, and it is claimed that the Powrwheel offers the lowest ground clearence and the most powerful drive unit of any comparable device currently available.

The concept of electric powered caravan movers is not new

When there is a drive wheel of some 2 inches diameter acting on a caravan tyre of about 22 inches diameter the combination results in a very low gear indeed, which, in turn, results in a massive amount of torque. So much so that I was shown a DVD in which a new 'Innovation' Powrwheel unit installed in a Bailey Pageant caravan which was hooked up to a two ton panel van, and the unmanned combined unit, weighting in excess of 3,000 Kgs, was reversed effortlessly up an incline.

A natural
accessory
for the
luxury
touring
caravan

The new 'Innovation' unit will gradually take over but at the time of writing both units are to be had.

A Powrwheel mover can be fitted on a new caravan by the dealership concerned, or retro-fitted by Powrwheel's agentys nationwide. For a single axle caravan the price will be somewhere between £800 and £1000. Twin axle units are also available.

I have found the device to be an absolute godsend and the company themselves to be not only outstandingly helpful, but a great pleasure to deal with. I recently found I had a problem with the handset for my unit, the afternoon before I wanted to use it. I phoned Powrwheel in Christchurch and spoke to a most knowledgeable and helpful technical bloke, who said 'I won't talk any longer because the post goes in ten minutes'. At 9 o'clock the following morning and 200 miles away, I received a replacement unit plus a helpful explanatory note. What more can I say? **See Useful Contacts at the back of the book.**

A point to note: If you are going to move the caravan on a battery-driven electric motor, the battery needs to produce a fair amount of 'wellie', so the van battery needs tobe a bit more robust than the run of the mill 60 or 76 amp hour. You should opt for a minimum power source of 100 amp hour. See **Chapter 5 - on 12 volt electrics.**

There are other, more modestly priced means of moving a caravan using 12 volt electricy, and one of these is the Mr Shifta at around £700. See photo on page 124.

It consists of a compact, battery driven wheeled trolley which has a 50mm. tow ball on top, at about the height of the tow ball on your car. It is steered by a long handle terminating in a crossbar which carries the forward and reverse twistgrip controls. See **Useful Contacts at the back of the book.**

The Mr Shifta is manoeuvred under the coupling head of the caravan, which is then lowered onto the trolley's towball by winding down the jockey wheel, the jockey wheel is then raised and the van can be moved in any direction by what is virtually a powerful electric tractor.

The brain child of an engineer of many years experience, the Mr Shifta Mark 1 came into being during the 1990s, and in 2000 was radically updated to produce Mr. Shifta 2, with twice the previous power. Its success stems partly from the powerful traction type battery employed, and partly from the different sized wheels available. The choice of wheel size obviously affects the gear ratio used in moving the load. Various tyre treads are also available, depending on the sort of terrain to be negotiated.

In February 2005 Mr Shifta Mk3 was launched. A further 25% of power is featured, plus improved 4 inch rear caster wheels with rubber tyres. These will make for easier handling prior to connecting to the caravan. The steering handle now folds to a vertical position for easier storage.

For those buying a secondhand Shifta, the plastic shell enclosing the unit was black on Mk 1, yellow on Mk 2, and the new Mk 3 is green, which makes for easy identification of the vintage.

A Powrwheel Caravan Mover has the plus factor of being permanently fitted to the caravan, so can be used when arriving on site; Mr Shifta is too heavy to take on holiday, so is restricted to use back at base.

Charging the Mr Shifta special traction battery calls for a few words of explanation. A traction battery is rated in a different way from a leisure battery; a 60 amp/hour traction battery would equate with about a 90 amp/hour leisure battery.

> Mr. Shifta is too heavy to take on holiday

It should be charged at a rate of about 10% of its capacity, so ideally one needs a 6-8 amp charger. Any charger between 5 and 10 amps would be appropriate.

What a traction battery does not like is to be trickle-charged after every short period of use by, say, a 2-3 amp charger. Far better to run the battery fairly well down, then charge at 5 amps or more for 14-16 hours.

This is the obvious point at which to mention a widely used method of taking the effort out of winding the corner steadies up and down with an electric wheel brace.

It consists of a metal rod about a foot long which has, at one end, a wheelbrace sized socket which fits the nut on the corner steadies. The rod is mounted into the chuck of an inexpensive cordless drill; the rod being hexagonal to prevent slippage in the chuck. I wouldn't be without my version of this labour saving item.

This useful little rod and socket is stocked by most caravan dealers' accessory shops.

Reverting briefly to the Mr Shifta if you keep your caravan at home, or anywhere where mains electricity is available, it would be in order to remove the leisure battery from the van, connect up the traction battery and use the on-board caravan charger for a good

7

overnight charge. The caravan charger is probably rated at about 4-5 amps, which would be adequate for a sustained period of charge.

Air Conditioning units have been around for a while, more often seen on up-market motor homes, and usually mounted on the roof. On a touring caravan, however, where we aim to keep the centre of gravity low, the roof is not the most ideal place to locate 100 lb of equipment. It would inevitably have some bearing on towing stability.

Electrolux, now known as Dometic, are among several manufacturers of rooftop air conditioning units. Various sizes are available, depending on the size of the caravan. On the smaller capacity units weights are coming down so that air conditioning can be had for a weight penalty of as little as 55-60 lb, or approx. 25 kg. For a 16-foot van or larger, however, a suitable unit would weigh up to 40 kg and this has to be included in the caravan's available payload.

Powering an air conditioner is another factor to consider. They are run off mains voltage current and so a pitch with a mains hook-up is a must. Consumption should not be a problem, since a typical unit would consume about the same as a camping type 750 watt electric kettle, ie just over 3 amps which should be acceptable on a modern campsite.

Truma have solved the weight-on-the-roof problem with their 'Frostair' units which are designed to be installed in under-bed lockers. The cold air is distributed through flexible trunking much the same as the blown hot air assemblies, all of which helps to keep the centre of gravity low down.

There are three models available, obviously related to the size of the caravan.

The Compact costs around £900, the Comfort around £970 and the Vario at £1299. The first two use about 2.8 amps and the big one takes 4.2 amps. Not cheap admittedly, but if you're holed up in Southern Spain in July you may well think it money well spent.

> **Air conditioning units could well become 'as standard'**

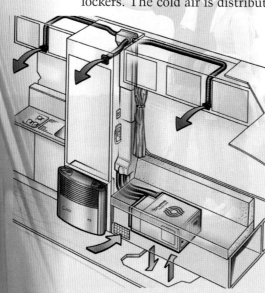

■ *Truma air conditioning layout*

Weights of Equipment (Payload)

Item	Weight (lb)	Kg
Awning (porch)	34	15
Awning (full)	42	19
Butane cylinder (4.5 kg size)	12 empty; 22 full	5.5 - 10
Ditto (7 kg size)	18 empty; 33 full	8 - 15
Battery (depending on size)	35	16
Spare wheel	30	13
Crockery/Cutlery (for 4) glasses, cooking pots	13 }	6
Fire extinguisher and blanket	4	1.8
Wood blocks and chocks	10	4.5
Bedding (per person approx.)	10	4.5
Clothing (per person approx.)	25	11
Books and games (approx.)	12	5.5
Folding chair (lightweight)	4	1.8
First-aid kit	2	0.9
Television	18	8.2
Hitchlock	6	2.7

How often have we returned to the caravan on a hot July afternoon in France (or England for that matter) to find it like an oven inside, and yearned for a bit of American technology?

I remember when the revolutionary Thetford built-in cassette loo was first shown at Earls Court, it was hailed as the best thing since sliced bread, and within a year practically every make of caravan and motor home had the cassette loo as original equipment. It would not surprise me to see a similar trend with air conditioning units. It is now standard in most cars. The weight is certainly a drawback, but for summer holiday comfort this is a significant piece of equipment, a natural accessory for the luxury touring caravan.

Allowing for two full 4.5 kg size gas cylinders, a full awning, clothing and bedding for three people, these items total about 300 lb or 135 kgs. Much of your personal luggage (quite a heavy item) will normally go in the car rather than in the caravan. I usually stow the awning in the car. Also there are various lightweight items not listed above, such as two 5-gallon water containers plus wastewater containers.

We are talking of approximately 3 cwt or 150 kg of gear to be loaded therefore, and it should not be difficult to settle on

Good air conditioning is money well spent

Onboard Equipment and Accessories

a caravan which can accept this, and conform with the target weights we have discussed earlier. You must do your own sums which will depend to a great extent on the size of your party and your car. Do be aware of your limits. Do not overload, ie do not exceed your **MLW** or **MTPLM**.

Do not accept the manufacturer's ex-works weight as gospel; it is quite often inaccurate. It may legally vary by up to plus or minus 5%. Find a public weighbridge and weigh the caravan empty – or better still, load up with all your gear and then weigh it.

Finally, you will have to be prepared to do your sums in either imperial or metric amounts. We are currently in a sort of twilight zone wherein what is left of the civilised world is steadily being bullied into centigrade, litres, kilometres, hectares, kilojoules and God knows what. Personally at my age I want none of it. I mean, imagine asking for 570 millilitres of Guinness. Meaningless. However, one cannot hold out against progress forever, and we are now calculating our caravan loading in kilos. So you might like a repeat of the little conversion table we gave in Chapter 1, in a slightly simpler form. To help you with your sums, remember

Remember to do your sums

$$1 \text{ kg} = 2.2. \text{ lb}$$
$$1 \text{ lb} = 0.45 \text{ kg}$$

Microwave

Finally, a thought about microwave ovens. In theory they can be used in a caravan fitted with mains electricity but whether or not to do so really needs some careful consideration. In an earlier edition, the Caravan Club's magazine En Route gave an excellent review of the pros and cons and made some of the following points'

The power output of an oven, expressed in watts, is not the same as the actual power consumed. In some cases the latter is more than double the former, and almost any microwave operated on a camp-site circuit where the load is restricted to 5 amp will certainly trip the installation's circuit breaker. Most Club sites will offer 16 amps per pitch, but other sites could offer less - maybe 10 amps or, on many continental sites, as little as 5 amps.

On continental sites the voltage is likely to be 220, rather than our 230 volts at home, and this could lower the microwave's performance to the point of making it virtually useless.

A simple formula for establishing how many watts may be consumed is that volts multiplied by amps equals watts. Therefore 230 volts x 10 amps equals 2300 watts. A continental circuit might be 220 volts x 5 amps, which equals 1100 watts. This is clearly quite a difference, and insufficient for most microwaves.

Microwave ovens are not designed to be shaken about or subjected to vibration. Towing could actually damage the unit, and with some models could invalidate the warranty.

Finally, there is the matter of weight. Most microwaves weigh around 50 lb or more - do you really need this extra burden?

A microwave oven fitted in a top-of-the-range caravan is a different matter. It will be designed to withstand towing and its weight will be included in the van's declared Mass in Running Order *(unladen weight)*.

These comments should be taken in context. We are discussing the advisability of taking with you the microwave from your kitchen without checking its suitability for caravan use. Many luxury caravans are fitted with microwaves as standard equipment, and these are obviously suitable for the job, although the problem of lower voltage abroad will still apply.

In general, then, microwave ovens should not be taken on holiday without prior serious consideration. Check all the facts, and consider whether a good tin opener and a saucepan might not be a better alternative.

A tin opener may be a better alternative

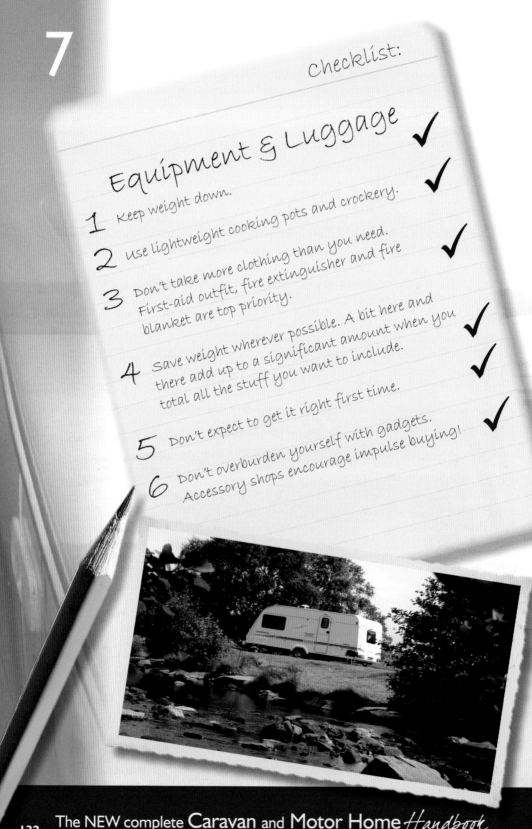

7

Checklist:

Equipment & Luggage ✓

1 Keep weight down. ✓

2 Use lightweight cooking pots and crockery. ✓

3 Don't take more clothing than you need.
First-aid outfit, fire extinguisher and fire ✓
blanket are top priority.

4 Save weight wherever possible. A bit here and
there add up to a significant amount when you ✓
total all the stuff you want to include. ✓

5 Don't expect to get it right first time.

6 Don't overburden yourself with gadgets.
Accessory shops encourage impulse buying! ✓

Caravan and Camping Sites in the U.K.

A great variety of caravan sites exists throughout the UK, many accommodating both tents and caravans and there are a number of guidebooks available listing camp and caravan sites by county.

I am reliably informed that there are now over five hundred thousand touring caravans in the UK, and if laid end to end, they would stretch from Lands End to John O'Groats **THREE TIMES**, which would really give Jeremy Clarkson something to worry about.

Quite a number of these are owned by folk who are not actually members of either the Camping & Caravanning Club or the Caravan Club. They do not, therefore receive copies of the clubs' site directories, although several club sites are open to non-members.

For non-members there is still a vast range of camping sites throughout the United Kingdom and indeed throughout Europe and beyond, up to and inside the Arctic circle. A number of specialist publishers provide information on these sites, often in great detail.

Obviously, number one on the list comes the companion volume to the **Caravanners Handbook, the Guide to Caravan and Camping Holidays**, also published by FHG Publications Ltd.

No site can buy its way into the guide

To mention two others, the **Alan Rogers Good Camps Guide** and **Cade's Camping and Touring Guide** have, between them, comprehensive coverage of sites in the UK and well over 20 European countries.

The Alan Rogers Guide runs to five volumes which cover most European countries. Quality is their main concern; all the listed sites have been visited and assessed. No site can 'buy in' to the listing, and every year, a few sites are dropped due to falling standards.

The Cade's Guide covers the UK - excluding Northern Ireland - and lists over 900 sites by county.

All these guide books are available from good bookshops, and in many cases are stocked by caravan dealers' accessory shops.

The Forestry Commission and the Camping and Caravanning Club added 21 new woodland sites to the club's list of over 100 warden-run sites.

So many beautiful sites with excellent facilities

If you are a tree person you will find the former Forestry Commission sites really are in the most attractive and tranquil settings. A tangible bonus is the 20% discount offered to Senior Citizens and disabled caravanners. This offer normally excludes the peak seasons of July and August, but five of their sites operate the discount throughout the year. It is worth sending for their well-produced brochure. (See Useful Contacts).

There are also sites in the ten National Parks in England and Wales. These are all areas of outstanding natural beauty, and the ten area authorities can provide details of the location of sites within the Parks. **These authorities are all listed in *Useful Contacts* at the back of the book**

The next chapter deals with the two principal clubs in more detail, but a few words here while on the subject of camping sites would be appropriate.

The Caravan Club and the Camping and Caravanning Club have much in common, in that both offer to members a large network of sites with excellent facilities. These usually include one or more toilet blocks which often include laundry, washing up and chemical toilet disposal facilities, all of which are maintained to a high standard.

The sites are warden controlled and various types of pitch are available. These vary between grass and hardstanding, with and without electric hook ups. An increasing number have 'super pitches' which have on-pitch connections for electricity, fresh and wastewater and TV aerial.

There are strict rules laid down governing occupancy of club sites and general behaviour, for the benefit of all concerned.

Some years ago, the Camping and Caravanning Club changed the title of their site wardens to Holiday Site Managers, which struck me as being unnecessarily pedantic, but there it is. Whatever they're called, they all do a fantastic job.

Each club has a large members only network of small privately owned sites, licensed for 5 caravans only, known as Certificated Locations *(Caravan Club)*, or Certificated Sites or Hideaways *(Camping and Caravanning Club)*. We have referred to these elsewhere.

Both clubs now offer facilities for members to pitch their vans permanently on a site either all the year round, or for the length of a summer season. Alternatively, some sites enable members to leave their vans in a secure compound, and bring them out on to a pitch as and when required, a facility known in France as *garage mort*. Prices vary, and are published by each club in their respective Sites Directories.

There are already hundreds of sites between the two clubs, and most may be booked in advance although it is not always necessary. Most commercial sites are open from March until the end of October, although some are open all the year. Many are set in attractive scenery, and usually offer excellent facilities by way of toilet, washroom, shower blocks and mains electricity.

Site wardens are truly the salt of the earth. Larger sites may have a number of assistant wardens, and they are all employed by the club. The smooth and efficient running of the site, the cleanliness and maintenance, the solution to all the members' queries and problems, these and a hundred other responsibilities are cheerfully dealt with by wardens and their patient, supportive partners.

We did once meet one exception on a Club site in the West Country, who had either been recruited from HM Prison Service, or he could have been an ex-drill sergeant from the Guards depot. He was abrupt, overbearing and short-tempered. To quote the late, great Francis Albert Sinatra, this guy was meaner 'n a junkyard dog. We left after two days, christened the site Stalag XIV and haven't been back since. He was strictly a one-off, however.

The greatest appeal for many Club members lies in the truly vast network of certificated locations throughout the country. Most, though not all, are on farms, where members are always sure of a warm welcome. Each location is licensed by the Club,

You have hundreds of sites to choose from

and is solely for the use of Club members. A certificated location or hideaway usually offers only basic facilities - a fresh water tap, a sewage disposal point and a dustbin.

Many offer fresh milk, eggs etc, but that's about all. Peace and quiet are the main features, but it is quite possible to tuck oneself away on a certificated site and yet be close to the facilities of a large town or seaside resort. The owner of a certificated location is allowed a maximum of only five caravans on the site at any one time, so you won't suffer if you're allergic to crowds.

An increasing number of certificated locations are installing mains hook-ups. This is in response to members who want the simplicity and tranquillity of a small rural site but still demand the hair dryer, electric toaster and all the comforts of home.

Personally I regret this tendency. We can all manage very well with our gas and our 12-volt batteries, and if this trend continues to the point where even a certificated location is an all-singing, all-dancing, miniature holiday camp, I think we shall buy a time-share in the Gobi desert. Perhaps I'm overreacting, but there are some things that are best kept simple.

Before leaving campsites, just a small titbit in passing. It was never my intention to list good sites which we know - the sites guides can do that, but a word about a gem of a location, especially for the Cornwall addicts. It's our favourite.

The Roseland Peninsula is on the south east coast of Cornwall and is more attractive, we feel, and less commercialised than the north, the surfing coast. At the south end of the Roseland, where the Percuil river flows into the Falmouth Roads, lies the unspoilt anchorage of St. Mawes. There's only one road in and out of this little town, and a couple of miles short of St Mawes the road passes through St. Just-in-Roseland. On the edge of St Just is the Trethem Mill Touring Park. Invisible from the road, this scenic, undulating site is unobtrusively and efficiently run by two generations of a kindly and helpful North Country family. There is a welcoming ambience about the place. If you want a bar, a disco, a take-away and karaoke on Saturdays, this is not the place. If you want a friendly, attractive, reasonably priced, peaceful site, with the most spotless loos north of Penzance, then try **Trethem Mill. Phone 01872 580504** for a well-illustrated brochure - *you won't be disappointed.*

Caravanning Abroad

When we talk of caravanning abroad we are talking in most cases about Europe. Further afield than this means either a long sea voyage, which with a caravan is fairly expensive, or a road journey of many thousands of miles.

Touring abroad? We recommend membership of a caravan club.

Many caravanners have toured in the UK for years with no help from either the caravanning clubs or the motoring organisations. Going 'foreign' is a rather different matter, and here I would strongly advise membership of one of the caravanning clubs.

They have vast experience of the needs, the wrinkles and procedures involved in taking your van across the water, They can book your ferries and your sites, if you wish. They can arrange your holiday insurance, including 'get home' recovery in the event of a breakdown or accident to either car, caravan or crew. They will supply you with your international camping carnet *(more of which later)*. They can supply you with sites guides for almost every country in Europe, including those which were, at one time, behind the Iron Curtain. They really are the experts.

You will find further reference in **Chapter 8** to the touring services, both home and abroad, offered by the Caravan Club and the Camping and Caravanning Club.

A couple of pages back we referred to the Alan Rogers camp sites guide. The Alan Rogers organisation, based in Kent offers a comprehensive travel service to caravanners heading for the Continent.

Over 225 inspected campsites can be pre-booked together with advantageous ferry deals.

Also linked to the Alan Rogers Travel Service is the rapidly expanding Camping Cheque organisation, which offers incredibly good value on European camping holidays.

Briefly, it consists of a loosely connected association of over 590 four and five-star campsites in 26 European countries, and these 590 include 15 naturist sites. Glossing over this nugget of information reminds me of a relevant quotation in which confidence is defined as having a full length mirror in the bathroom. However, let us not get sidetracked. Camping Cheque can offer some excellent savings on ferry crossings with Norfolk Line and really outstanding bargains at 4 and 5 star continental camp sites for those caravanners who can holiday during the off-peak season. Off-peak effectively means any time except July and August. I know that excludes many families with school-age children, but it still leaves a large body of caravanners who are free to please themselves.

Bargain prices are indeed just that - sometimes half normal price, and remember, these are all top-quality sites, usually with swimming pools and all the facilities one would expect from a 4- and 5-star site.

From the Kent office you can buy however many nights camping you require for *(currently)* £11.95 per night, which covers two

Bargains do exist especially during the off-peak season

people plus car and caravan **AND ELECTRIC HOOK-UP.** You buy your camping cheques before leaving the UK, and they are accepted at any of the participating sites throughout Europe.

On top of this, many of the participating sites offer discounts, eg 7 nights for 6 cheques. **See Useful Contacts at the back of the book.**

A very similar scheme is operated by Touring Cheque, who offer virtually identical discounts for low season camping in top class sites in 10 European countries.

Phone 08703 667828 for details, or visit **www.touringcheque. co.uk. See** *Useful Contacts* **at the back of the book** for Alan Rogers Travel Service, also Camping Cheque.

Good driving? A mixture of good manners and common sense

Most European sites offer mains hook-up and toilet facilities. Many have a camp provisions shop, and perhaps a takeaway cooked food service, a bar and a swimming pool. Some are a great deal more basic, and the various sites guides give a fairly accurate description of what you may expect to find.

The Caravan Club's two-volume European sites guide often gives details of sites, which are the result of reports from members who have visited the location previously.

Touring in Europe offers a very wide variety of sites. Having found the coastal resort or location you want, you may well find a site two or three miles inland is considerably cheaper and less crowded, and is well worth the short drive to the beach. Also, don't be put off by sites with ratings of only one or two stars - they won't have a swimming pool, but the facilities are usually very good value for money.

Often the municipal sites, as distinct from privately owned ventures, can also be well run, quite adequate and represent keen value for money.

When on the road, driving on the right will need some extra concentration to begin with. Moving away from the kerb, turning left at junctions and overtaking also need particular care but one gets used to it quite quickly. The Caravan Club's Continental Sites Guide and Directory has a comprehensive section at the beginning of the book on international traffic signs. Many of these are common to our road signs in the UK, but do study them thoroughly before you go. Ignoring traffic signs in your host country may well involve you in an on-the-spot fine, and being a 'foreigner' is not usually an effective excuse.

In the earlier remarks on towing in general, we made the point about extended door mirrors since the width of the caravan will make the existing door mirrors virtually useless.

We spoke of the need to keep a constant eye on the offside door mirror, so as not to be caught napping when being overtaken by large lorries. When driving on the right, the offside of your outfit is the left side. I personally would not tow at all without extension mirrors on both sides, although many caravanners make do with only one, on the right or offside *(in the UK)*. Abroad, an extension mirror on the left is absolutely vital, particularly since your driving seat is on the 'wrong' side. Some countries make extension mirrors on both sides mandatory, it is certainly so in Spain. The Spanish police are very hot on this point, and failure to comply results in a hefty on-the-spot fine. Law or no law, extension mirrors on both sides is simply common sense.

Good driving, as we know, is just a mixture of good manners and common sense, and towing abroad without a good side mirror on the left shows not only a lack of common sense, it is downright stupid.

The Caravan Club's Sites Guide and Directory carries a wealth of information on motoring country by country, together with information on currency, weather, public holidays, obligatory documents and equipment for car and caravan, indeed every possible scrap of information you could need for travelling abroad. The Camping and Caravanning Club can supply you with similar information through their associated club, the RAC.

Correct documents whilst abroad is essential

Naturally, when travelling abroad, you need passports for every member of the party. On 10-year passports, husband and wife now need separate passports, as do children of 16 and over. Visas are not required in EU countries but are necessary in some Eastern European countries. A telephone call to the London Tourist Office or the Embassy of your chosen country will clarify any questions on visas.

Remember to take the registration document for your car. If it is not your own vehicle, eg a company car, you must have a letter authorising you to take the car abroad on holiday. A 'green card' *(from the vehicle insurers)* is not essential in EU countries but you are strongly advised to carry one, and do make sure that your insurers know that you are towing a caravan. This applies both at home and abroad.

Health problems when abroad are best covered by either one of the two clubs, who are probably arranging the travel aspect of your holiday anyway.

At one time the caravanner in Europe covered most likely problems by applying for a form E111 from a post office, and this gave one the access to the national health facilities in the country to be visited. The care available with a form E111 has recently been scaled down somewhat and it is now prudent to arrange an effective level of cover through either a travel agent or one of the clubs.

Another important document is a camping carnet, which has recently been renamed 'camping card international'. This is like a camper's passport and is available from either of the caravanning clubs. At a continental campsite, the site office will retain your card throughout your stay, rather than holding on to your passport which could make for difficulties when cashing cheques.

Finance abroad is now simpler than in the days of travellers cheques and foreign currency. Euros are now very widely used and can be obtained in advance from many sources including the Post Office, and usually free of commision.

Maestro and Visa cards are acceptable at literally thousands of facilities abroad.

Don't forget Ireland. Guiness in every post office

The point has been made elsewhere that all travel details can be arranged by either the Caravan Club Red Pennant service or the Camping and Caravanning Club's Carefree service - **See Chapter 9**. If all this sounds a bit involved believe me, it isn't. The opportunities to see other countries, people and climates, to enjoy wide varieties of scenery and the *(usually)* quieter roads for travelling, all combine to make the simple paperwork more than worthwhile.

The whole continent of Europe is just down the road. There are ferries sailing from ports all around the coasts of England, Wales and Scotland. These connect us with every part of Europe's coastline, stretching from Scandinavia in the north to Spain in the south and west, and of course, with Ireland.

When making plans to cross the water, don't forget either Northern Ireland or the Republic of Ireland. Don't be put off by the troubles which used to beset that beautiful country. The Irish are peace-loving, hospitable and very friendly people, and both north and south have some indescribably lovely scenery, with miles of near-deserted roads. Where else but Ireland could you be sure of getting a pint of draught Guinness in almost any post office? A very civilised way to live.

Go down to the southwest, spend a week or so in the utter peace of the Ring of Kerry. You will remember the holiday for the rest of your days.

A comprehensive list of camping sites in Ireland (Ulster and Eire) is available from the Irish Caravan and Camping Council, PO Box 4443, Dublin 2. or visit their website at www.campingireland.ie.. This is an excellent guide, lavishly illustrated with photographs and maps, and the two British Caravan Clubs can help with details of the sea crossings to Ireland.

Finally, there will always be someone to help you find your way around when abroad; perhaps other English families who have already been there for some time and have all the local information sorted out. English caravanners who would merely exchange a cautious nod on a site in Cornwall tend to fall upon each other with joyful cries upon meeting on foreign soil. You should have no difficulty in recognising your fellow Brits abroad. The women wear bras, the men wear socks and the kids drop litter.

caravan Sites

1 Sites vary - either privately and commercially run, or run by or approved by the Caravan Club, or the Camping and Caravanning Club. ✓

2 Commercial sites tend to be medium to large. Facilities are usually good and include toilets, showers and a shop, and maybe a swimming pool, bar, clubroom, take-away, children's playroom etc. ✓

3 Club sites or locations can be large with comprehensive facilities, or five-van only affairs with a tap and a dustbin. ✓

4 The larger the site the better the facilities generally, and of course the larger the crowds. ✓

5 Peace, quiet and comparative solitude means joining one of the caravan clubs. Five-van sites are for members only. ✓

6 Good sites exist also in National Parks. Going abroad? Either of the caravanning clubs or the Alan Rogers Travel Service can provide detailed European sites guides, and arrange all ferry bookings, travel insurance etc. ✓

7 See that your family and pets behave as you would want others around you to behave. Remember, when abroad we are all British ambassadors. ✓

The Camping and Caravanning Club

One cannot write a book about caravanning without detailing the activities of the two principal clubs.

Located in Coventry, the Camping and Caravanning Club was the first such Club in the world and its origins trace back to 1901. In that year six cyclists held the first meeting of the Association of Cycle Campers. Throughout the years the organisation has grown until today it has over 500,000 members. As well as touring caravanners the Club welcomes motor caravanners, trailer tenters and tenters in to membership.

The Club has a network of over 100 sites throughout the UK. Nearly all sites offer full facilities which include mains electric hook-ups, toilet block(s) with showers, dishwashing and laundry facilities, chemical toilet disposal points and, in some cases, a number of hard-standing pitches, a games/television room and a dog walking area.

So many wonderful sites So little time to see them

The majority of sites are open to non-members. There are special deals for families with children and for those aged over 55. All the Club's own sites are described in a colourful book, Your Place in the Country, which is updated and sent to all members free every year.

Each entry carries a photograph and description of the site, camping charges, notes on local features and information on opening and closing dates, although a few sites are open all year round.

The Camping and Caravanning Club

The friendly Club

The Club publishes another site guide, Your Big Sites Book and this lists more than 4,500 caravan sites in Britain. Included in Your Big Sites Book are about 1200 small sites known as 'Certificated Sites'. These are all in rural settings, often on farms, may only accommodate a maximum of five caravans at one time, and are strictly for members only. The more quiet and secluded of these five-van sites are known as 'Hideaways'. Also listed

9

in Your Big Sites Book is virtually every licensed and commercial campsite in Britain. Many people reckon this is the best and most comprehensive UK sites guide available.

The Club organises around 300 Temporary Holiday Sites each year, which are run by Club members for Club members and offer economic and friendly camping all over Britain. The Club also has a nationwide network of District Associations. There are about 100 of these, grouped under 13 larger regions. Members may join their local District Association, or one of their choice further away.

In addition to these regional and district groups, there are a number of 'special interest' sections, including photographic, folk dance and song, mountain activity, canoe-camping and a boating section. All these sections have a full programme of activities and are well supported. Membership of each involves a small extra subscription to cover administration.

Photographic, folk dance, mountain activity and a host of other interests available

For members who are new to caravanning, the Club runs a number of weekend practical caravan handling and manoeuvring courses at locations throughout the country, as does the Caravan Club. The Camping and Caravanning Club's courses include both theory and practice, covering subjects such as towing law, relative weights of car and van, correct loading, use of electricity and gas plus hands-on practice of hitching up and siting the van, and the oft-dreaded and thorny problem of confident reversing.

In cooperation with the Institute of Advanced Motorists, the Club runs courses which will enable a member to take and pass the IAM advanced caravan handling and trailer towing qualification. Well worth the effort.

The Club does not publish a continental sites guide, but it can supply guides to most European countries published by sister clubs in those countries. The French guide for instance published by the French Federation of Camping and Caravanning Clubs lists more than 11,000 sites in France.

The Club also offers insurance services for caravans, cars, motor caravans, household cover, tents and camping equipment, plus, of course, travel insurance and cover for pets and small boats. In addition to these services the Club automatically covers each member for £500,000 worth of public liability. It also has an excellent technical advice service to caravanners, on all aspects of caravanning.

Instant cover on the Club's insurance policies can be arranged online through the Club's website.

Other services available to Club members are discounted car sales *(new and used)*, breakdown cover for car and caravan arranged in conjunction with the RAC, a local and national telephone weather forecasting service and an unsecured loan service at attractive rates of interest.

There is a colourful monthly magazine circulated to members which contains a good cross-section of interesting caravan-related advertisements, articles of general and technical interest, news of sites and places to visit. Foreign touring, nature conservation and members' letters are all featured.

The Camping and Caravanning Club has recently introduced another service to members, in the shape of a review of towcars from several different aspects which, it must be said, is taking a leaf out of the Caravan Club's book, and why not? The features and functions of both clubs are similar to a great extent. Unless one were a member solely of the Caravan Club the advice on towcars would not be available to Camping and Caravanning Club members, but that has now been rectified. I have heard criticism of the 'Friendly Club' as the Camping and Caravanning Club likes to be called for emulating this analysis of towcars but the great majority of services offered by each club is to be found in the other, and this additional service makes sense. I still think it is worth having membership of both.

The Camping and Caravanning Club's current subscription is £36.00 plus £10.00 joining fee waived for direct debit. If annual subscriptions are pledged through direct debit, or through a credit card on an ongoing basis, the £10.00 joining fee is waived. The address and telephone number of the Club's headquarters in Coventry can be found under **Useful Contacts**, also the Club website.

www.campingandcaravanningclubco.uk

The Caravan Club

The Caravan Club was founded in 1907 and caters for the needs and interests of all caravanners, including folding and motor home owners.

In terms of numbers, the membership is similar to that of the Camping and Caravanning Club, and includes caravanners, motor home members and trailer tenters. It also has the largest network of Club caravan sites in Britain.

THE
CARAVAN
CLUB

9

Although many of these services provided for members are similar to those offered by the Camping and Caravanning Club, each has its own character and unique features and the two clubs complement each other rather than compete as do, for example, the AA and the RAC. Each needs the other really, for if there were only one club, the membership would be unwieldy and the incentive to improve services would be gone.

The Caravan Club is based at East Grinstead, West Sussex, where a large specialist staff functions most efficiently. Expert technical advice is available to members on every aspect of caravanning. There is a legal helpline, and also a personal loan service and credit card scheme, both of which operate through Frizzell Bank Ltd.

An excellent foreign touring department is a feature of The Caravan Club; their 'Red Pennant' travel insurance is hard to beat. Ferry bookings, continental site reservations, escorted holidays, caravanning package deals, comprehensive insurance cover designed to cope with every imaginable touring misfortune - all are available on terms which compare favourably with those of the motoring organisations. From personal experience I can vouch for the cheerful efficiency of the ladies of the Red Pennant department.

Insurance, legal helpline, personal loans and credit card schemes available to members

The Caravan Club publishes its own monthly members' magazine. This is a mine of interesting and practical articles, plus advertisements, correspondence and information covering the whole spectrum of caravanning.

The Club also has an insurance department which offers a wide range of cover to members - *see Insurance section in **Chapter 10***. In addition to the usual caravan and motor caravan cover, the Club offers a 'Hitchfree' policy which is a purely personal cover for travelling abroad without either car or caravan. Useful for either business or pleasure travel, it is part of the Red Pennant service. Motor insurance and Home insurance are also available to members.

An important function fulfilled by The Caravan Club is the maintenance of 'Theftcheck', a computerised register of members' caravans, with chassis numbers. Police forces throughout the country make frequent use of these records when dealing with stolen caravans.

Another most useful function for caravanners is fulfilled by the Caravan Club in that they are joint sponsors, with the Camping and Caravanning Club and the National Caravan Council, of the nationwide Approved Caravan Workshops scheme **see *Chapter 12* on maintenance**.

To be members of the scheme a dealer's workshop has to reach a high standard of practical, technical and business efficiency, which involves thorough vetting by qualified engineers. Regular re-inspections are part of the scheme and the end product is that owners can be absolutely confident that the important servicing of their caravan is in proven proficient and ethical hands.

A breakdown and recovery service called 'Mayday' is available to Club members, which operates in conjunction with Green Flag National Breakdown. The scheme covers solo cars and motor homes as well as caravan outfits. One should note that, unlike the AA and RAC breakdown schemes, the Club scheme covers the vehicle rather than the driver.

9

A big event in the Club diary is the Towcar of the Year Awards, which the Caravan Club has sponsored for some years now.

Currently seven different types of car are judged on performance and 'caravanability', and an overall winner is chosen from the seven class winners. Full results are published in the Club's magazine, and provide a most useful guide to selecting a towcar.

As The Camping and Caravanning Club has its District Associations, so The Caravan Club has its local Centres. Centres hold frequent rallies and social events throughout the country and the club magazine always carries a section devoted to local Centre activities.

If you are drawn by the prospect of a field full of fellow caravanners from your own patch, assembled in a great gregarious gathering, drinking each other's coffee and admiring their gadgets and installations, then join your local Centre. The address and phone number of each Centre's Rally Secretary are listed in the supplement to the Club's Sites Directory and Handbook.

If peace and quiet are more your scene you have access, through the Club's Sites Guide, to nearly 3,000 Certificated Locations (CLs), which are scattered nationwide.

British and European directories available - very useful

As with The Camping and Caravanning Club's Certificated Sites and 'Hideaways', CLs are strictly for five caravans only and for the use of members only. Basic facilities are the usual order, although many CLs are now providing mains electric hook-ups.

Unlike The Camping and Caravanning Club, The Caravan Club does not have categories of membership specialising in different kinds of activity, but they do list certificated locations where different facilities and activities can be found locally. These are grouped under the separate headings of fishing, golf and horse riding. There is also a list of CLs where Bed and Breakfast are available. A useful feature of the Sites Directory is the listing of these CLs by category of activity and geographically by county.

The Sites Directory also lists some 200 established sites run by The Club. These are all warden-controlled, have good facilities by way of toilet and shower blocks, and the majority of individual pitches are now equipped with mains hook-ups. Some sites have hard-standings and designated motor caravan waste disposal points. Several sites are open throughout the year, and some are open to non-members.

The Directory is revised and issued free to members every two years. The current edition also serves as a members handbook. It has been greatly improved, with a colour coded directory of Club sites and certificated locations by counties. An invaluable part of the book has information on Club bye-laws, lists of caravan dealers, legal requirements on towing, details of 12-volt electrics and much more. This is the most informative and comprehensive club handbook yet. Excellent - well worth joining for.

The club also publishes a comprehensive European sites directory in two parts. 'Caravan Europe' part 1 covers France, Spain, Portugal and Andorra, part 2 covers the rest of Europe. Cost to members is £9.50 for Part 1, £9.00 for part 2, and £16.00 for both, plus post & packing in each case. Both contain much helpful advice for each country, varying from traffic signs to currency.

These two continental sites guides have to be purchased from the Club, whereas the UK Sites Guide is free. They are not expensive, and the wide range of information is invaluable.

If you are new to caravanning or motor caravanning and are a little reluctant to tow or handle your new acquisition on the Queen's highway, then fear not. The Club runs a series of really helpful one or one-and-a-half day courses on practical caravan handling and manoeuvring, at various centres around the country. They are held from March to November, also open to non-members, and all details can be had from the Club's Events department.

The Caravan Club annual subscription is currently £37.00 with a £7.50 joining fee. The joining fee, however, is waived if you opt to pay your annual subscription by direct debit or through a credit card on an ongoing basis. Family membership is £3, which is only necessary if other members of the family wish to use Club facilities during the absence of the full member.

If you are to get really full value from your hobby, then you should certainly join one of the two caravanning clubs. Their services and wealth of experience will make your holidays so much more enjoyable and easy to organise. Many caravanners are members of both clubs, Herself and me included. And why not? The truly vast and varied range of attractive locations which are available only to members more than justifies the reasonable cost.

The National Caravan Council

The National Caravan Council, or NCC as it is widely known throughout the caravan industry, is a trade association. As such it is close to being unique in the UK, as its membership comprises companies and individuals from every part of the caravan industry - manufacturers, dealers, distributors, park owners and a vast range of suppliers of specialist products and services (*everything*

9

To get full value from caravanning you should join at least one of the main clubs

9

from finance houses to manufactures of small, but vital, pieces of caravan equipment). Few other trade bodies can command such a wide range of representation.

The NCC also covers every type of leisure and residential vehicle known by various Acts of Parliament as a 'caravan'. From tourers, through motor motor homes and caravan holiday-homes to residential park homes, this requires the NCC staff and members to keep ahead of technical, commercial, legal and regulatory developments, not just within the UK but also in Europe. So, there's depth as well as breadth.

NATIONAL CARAVAN COUNCIL LIMITED

How does all this come together for the benefit of the caravanning public, since they are the only ones who don't appear to be members? The NCC works through highly specialised committees of its own members, giving up their own valuable business time, and with outside agencies - such as British Standards, Corgi, two caravanning clubs, HPI, Government departments and Brussels *(the list seems endless).*

The aim of all this is to ensure, through constantly improving Standards and Codes of Practice, that caravans in the UK are made, sold, serviced, towed, lived in and generally looked after, with the wellbeing of the caravanner at heart.

Quality, safety and security are paramount. Quite a tough battle, but not perhaps for an organisation in which one member can frequently find himself across the table from another NCC member with diametrically opposed views. Tough negotiation is a regular theme.

The NCC has been around for over 60 years but it is far from being an institution. It was one of the few trade associations in the UK to win government funding in 1996 to set up its own Internet website, which may be reached at www.nationalcaravan. co.uk. So it sees itself as being in touch with the general caravanning public and is constantly looking for ways to improve communication. Any caravanner is welcome to approach the NCC at its Directorate Headquarters in Aldershot when seeking to resolve a problem or merely to ask for advice. Equally, you will probably find most NCC members just as helpful, since they all have the interests of the caravanner at heart. The NCC address and telephone number are listed at the end of the book under **Useful Contacts**.

Owners Clubs

Most caravan manufacturers, **Swift**, **Elddis**, **Bailey** etc have an owners club whose membership consists of caravanners owning that particular brand of van. The clubs are not administered by the manufacturers, but are self governing with a secretary, chairman etc., and most of them hold rallies and social events.

There are probably more owners clubs devoted to marques which have ceased trading than those whose names are still current, some going back many years. Names and locations of club secretaries can be obtained from any of the national caravan magazines.

The Historic Caravan Club

The owners clubs described above are too numerous to list, but the Historic Caravan Club deserves a special mention.

The Club was formed over ten years ago for enthusiasts of pre-1961 trailer caravans and the horse drawn ancestors of the touring caravan.

Their Chairman is currently Paul Genner. **See** *Useful Contacts*, and I am indebted to Paul for the photograph of the 1927 Eccles which I mentioned in **Chapter 1**.

The Club is a member club of the Association of Caravan and Camping Exempted Organisations and also a member club of the Federation of British Historic Vehicle Clubs.

Over 100 award-winning camp sites

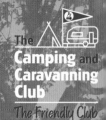

General Hints

This is just a collection of small tips and suggestions to help you enjoy caravanning, and perhaps make life simpler. Old hands could doubtless double the list, but perhaps they will also be able to pick up the odd point that hadn't occurred to them before.

Soft Furnishings

Many a second-hand caravan can be greatly improved inside by some new curtains and/or loose covers. One of our earlier caravans was bought new. We chose it because it had the features we wanted at the price we could afford, and it 'felt right', but it was spoilt by skimpy, dreary curtains. Herself tracked down some attractive material in the local market, and made up more generous curtains which transformed the interior appearance.

If you replace curtains or upholstery fabrics, do remember to treat them with a fire retardant spray. Since the early '90s, furnishings in caravans will have been so treated, but it's worth noting that this safety treatment will not survive more than two or three washings. In this case do re-spray them yourself.

> Treat replaced upholstery with a fire retardant spray

Good quality soft furnishings are worth preserving, particularly when they are subjected to use by a rampage of children. It is surprising what can be dropped or spilled on seats during a fortnight. Washable loose covers are well worth either making or buying. There are always adverts for loose cover services in the caravan magazines.

■ *Attractive upholstery in Bailey's budget Ranger*

Protection from Insects

On an earlier caravan, we had anti-mosquito nets over all our opening windows, including the skylight. Netting *(again from the local market)* was fastened over the window openings with 2-inch long strips of Velcro sewn to the net and the corresponding pieces stuck to the wall around the opening with Evo-stik. On hot summer nights when the windows were open, these were invaluable.

A modern caravan will almost certainly be already fitted with insect-screen blinds on all windows and roof vents. To buy these complete and fit them yourself is an expensive and tedious task. The net and Velcro system is both economical and effective.

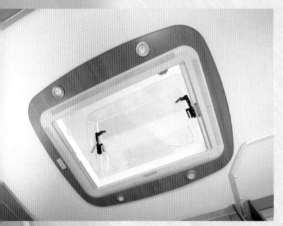

We also use a hanging curtain, consisting of 1-inch wide coloured strips of plastic, in the door opening. It is fixed by small hooks and screw eyes above the door, and it really does keep the flies out. Again, a modern caravan may well be fitted with a fly-screen door.

Ventilation

Talking of fresh air brings us to the subject of ventilators. On chilly evenings it is tempting to stuff odd socks and tea towels into the ventilators and work up a good old fug. Don't do it. The ventilators are essential for safety, particularly if you have a gas heater or a fridge in operation. Ventilators are usually set at floor level and they ensure an adequate supply of essential fresh air. Should you be unfortunate enough to have a gas leak, the ventilators will do much to disperse the gas which will accumulate at floor level. Inadequate ventilation could result in a literally lethal explosion.

Uninvited guests are easily kept out with net and Velcro.

Laundry

You will find that a length of clothesline and some pegs are useful on a summer holiday. The need to wash the odd 'smalls' and tea towels, or to dry swimsuits and towels, always arises. It is a simple matter to rig a temporary clothesline, perhaps between van and car or even in the awning. *(On a sunny day an awning can work up quite a formidable temperature.)*

Having said this, the need for in-van laundry rarely arises. Most established campsites, as distinct from 5 van certificated locations, have up to date toilet blocks. These usually include a laundry room, often with coin-operated washing machine and spin drier facilities.

Tyres

Before setting off always check your car and caravan tyre pressures. Check them when cold, not when you stop for fuel. You should frequently examine your van tyres for signs of splitting or cuts - not only the treads, but also the side walls. Accidental 'kerbing' can damage a tyre to the point of potential danger.

Unlike car tyres, the tyres on a caravan suffer very little tread wear, it is the tyre walls which gradually weaken and deteriorate. Unfortunately this often tends to go unnoticed.

We made the point, when discussing second-hand caravans, that the safe life of a caravan tyre is about five years. This is another point which often gets overlooked. We shall go further into the subject of tyre safety. *See Chapter 12 on Maintenance.*

Tyron Safety Bands

If you have a blow out at speed, snaking usually follows, which in turn tends to rip the deflated tyre off the wheel completely. This, in turn can often cause the caravan to overturn, and this is a thoroughly unpleasant experience. Apart from the possible involvement of other vehicles, the caravan is usually a complete write-off.

If, after rapid deflation of the tyre, the van remains upright, then usually little harm is done. The difference between these two incidents is frequently down to whether or not the deflated tyre parts company with the wheel. This is where the Tyron safety band comes in.

If you look at a car or caravan wheel minus its tyre, you will see that the rims at the edge of the wheel stand up much higher than the hollowed out well in the centre. The circumference of the wheel at the rims is much greater than it is around the well in the centre.

If this well were not there, it would be impossible to fit the tyre on to the wheel. Unfortunately the well also makes it easy for a deflated tyre to come off the wheel, particularly if there is some sideways force on the tyre, as in snaking.

The Tyron safety band is a metal band which goes around the circumference of the wheel, covering over the well in the centre. This prevents the beads on the tyre from dropping into the well, prior to the tyre coming off altogether. With Tyron safety bands, the wheel rims will not come into contact with the road, even after full deflation, because the tyre is kept in its correct position by the safety band, which enables the caravan to be brought to a safe stop.

The above description may be a little difficult to visualise, so make a point of seeing the short continuous video film on Tyron safety bands. This is on display at many caravan dealerships, and clearly demonstrates the principles involved.

Leaflets are also available and the Tyron safety bands can be fitted to your caravan wheels at any dealer's workshop.

They can be transferred easily when changing vans, and in terms of potential safety and peace of mind they are money well spent.

It should be noted that when purchasing Tyron Safety Bands for your caravan wheels, you receive a Tyron Customer Care Kit. This should be carried at all times when towing. It is quite compact and includes a number of small items including an Allen key. A garage would need this to enable them to remove and replace a tyre in the event of a puncture.

Wheel Nuts

Keep Allen keys to hand - just in case

Check also your van wheel nuts for tightness; use a decent sized wheel brace, not the brace used for winding down the corner steadies. Better still, invest in a torque wrench, to ensure correct tightness without overtightening. This should be at a torque setting of about 60lb/ft for nuts screwed on to wheel studs and 65lb/ft for bolts which go through the wheel and screw into the brake drum.

Incidents of caravans losing a wheel en route are by no means uncommon. Extremely dangerous and potentially costly, this hazard can be safely guarded against by correct checking and tightening. We referred to both tyres and torque wrenches *in the 'Towing on the road' section of Chapter 2.*

Spare Wheel

We said earlier that many modern caravans have large lockers at the front, to contain gas cylinders plus spare wheel. This makes for a lot of extra nose-weight. A few enlightened caravan manufacturers supply a locker at the rear end of the caravan for the spare wheel. This is an excellent solution to the problem, as long as you remember not to have too much weight behind the caravan's axle, since this contributes towards swaying or snaking on the move. If you stow the spare at the tail end, do remember to balance your loading so as to achieve a correct nose-weight.

Safe & Secure Products of Bristol - *see Useful Contacts* - market a very good spare wheel carrier which fits underneath the van,

between the two main chassis members. It fits the majority of Al-Ko, Knott and BPW chassis, using standard locating holes, so no need for drilling.

The steel carrier is zinc plated against road salt corrosion, can be security locked, and is reversible to make the spare wheel accessible from either side, for continental towing. It fits just behind the axle, which is an ideal location for the extra weight of a spare wheel. That's where ours goes and I thoroughly recommend this accessory. Admittedly it is a chore to have to grovel under the van with an air line when checking the spare tyre pressure, and there is occasionally the vague dread that some forecourt rally driver is going to motor over one's legs while thus engaged. I have survived so far however, and still think it's one of the best answers to spare wheel storage.

Alternatively, the spare can be checked, without crawling under the caravan, by unlocking the carrier and extending the 'trombone' tubes, which will bring the spare wheel out to the edge of the van.

The assembly comes in for a fair amount of road spray in wet weather, so it is recommended that the trombone-style tubes are separated at least once a year, and thoroughly greased.

Al-Ko also produce a similar spare wheel carrier designed to fit their chassis.

New caravans which are delivered with a spare wheel are slowly on the increase, but, oh dear, when will ALL manufacturers realise that most buyers would willingly stand the cost of this?

What chance would a car dealer have of selling a car without a spare? Not only that, but a recent reader's letter to a caravan magazine made the point that along with the spare wheel should go a wheel brace and a jack. Well, why not?

Remember to include the weight of the spare wheel when loading

10

Positioning Your Caravan

In *Chapter 2* on siting your caravan, I mentioned positioning the outfit so that in a strong wind the awning is on the sheltered side of the caravan. Some shelter from wind can also be gained by positioning the van behind a wall or clump of bushes, but in this connection try to avoid parking actually underneath trees. Various species of tree can drip sticky substances on to caravan and awning which take a lot of removing; birds will most effectively do the same thing.

If you are holidaying on the west coast of Scotland for example, or indeed on many continental coast sites, there could well be quite a strong prevailing wind. Don't site your caravan so that you present the side of the van *(opposite to the awning)* square on to the wind. This will cause your caravan to rock about. Site your outfit about 45 degrees away from the prevailing wind so that a corner of the caravan is presented to the wind, thus offering much less resistance.

Consider the birds'n'trees when siting your caravan

When siting, consider also the path of the sun. Wind and other considerations permitting, you will want to see as much of the sun as possible. Having set up your camp with awning rigged and pegged down all round, it is a bit depressing to find you would be much better off with the whole lot rotated through 90 degrees.

In-van Entertainment

What is the first thing most caravanners do having arrived on site, disconnected car and van, and wound down the corner steadies? Well, in our case, Herself slings out the water containers and trolley and I trek off to tank up with fresh water. While I'm gone, Herself stows the food, booze and assorted goodies we have brought with us, then when I return with the water, we make a pot of tea. Not a word is spoken; we both know our tasks.

In recent years we have noted the emergence of an altogether different routine among some of our neighbours. Once the steadies are wound down, the lady of the outfit is sent packing to fetch water while the gent in charge fishes out and assembles a large collapsible metal mast. The first time I saw this happen I looked round, unsuccessfully, for the sailing dinghy.

No, what I was watching was the assembly of a television aerial which, when erected, would have done credit to any NATO country's early warning system. By now, the First Mate is back with the water, and she is inside, critically viewing the TV while bellowing instructions to the gent who is rotating the ironmongery to get the best reception.

These ominous looking erections can be inserted in the jockey wheel socket, having first removed the jockey wheel assembly, or they can be supported by a maze of guy ropes.

This whole routine can be bypassed by having one of several models of omni-directional aerials fixed to the caravan roof. These are now standard equipment on most new caravans, and are internally wired with coaxial cable to an aerial socket somewhere in the sitting area.

Television reception on portable sets varies considerably between sites. One of the problems of the long-distance caravanner is having to tune the set to local transmitters, but there are portable sets now available on which this chore is greatly reduced. Caravan dealer accessory shops often carry a wide range of TVs, and local tuning is a point to raise when buying a set for the van.

'Status' is a rapidly expanding brand of radio and television antennae for caravans. They are marketed and made in the UK by Grade UK Ltd.

The Status 315 'flying saucer' aerial with the spike on top is a familiar sight today, fitted as original equipment on many caravans. This is an omni-directional aerial which requires no adjustment. There are many UK locations, however, where TV reception is below standard, so for the fastidious viewer, the Status 530 is the answer. An adjustable, directional aerial, it is mounted through the roof on a pole which terminates in the caravan wardrobe. It can therefore be adjusted from inside the van for height, direction and vertical/horizontal mode. Retail price is currently around £125, with a shorter pole version at £110. Both the 315 and 530 models are used with a 12/24 volt power booster, which also includes connection for a radio aerial.

The company also market a neat folding, portable set-top antenna, This is available in UK only form or for world-wide use.

*Contact Grade UK Ltd - **see** Useful Contacts* for detailed brochures.

If you prefer to listen to music in your caravan as opposed to watching the television, do consider going a step further than a portable radio. Reception on portables inside a metal-clad van is not always ideal. Fitting a car cassette/radio unit or CD player

Consider fitting a music system for the best results

10

with an internal aerial and stereo speakers is a simple task for the average DIY person. Overhead lockers, cupboards and/or shelves will house one of these very compact and neat units, and likewise the speakers. Do make sure you have a suitable in-line fuse in the supply wire from your terminal block in the caravan.

Car accessory shops sell an internal aerial which will fit neatly to the inside of a caravan window. Small and neat, it needs a 12-volt supply which powers a small amplifier. This boosts the signal received by the aerial.

We have one of these for our caravan radio, it avoids cutting holes in the van body for a car type aerial and provides really good reception. I can strongly recommend it.

Portable radios are often plagued at night by interference from the fluorescent strip-lights in the van. This can be cured by fitting strip-lights which are specially suppressed against radio interference; alternatively, an inexpensive suppressor kit is marketed by Lab Craft, available from caravan dealers.

A portable Larder - always welcome

On the subject of radio and TV, don't annoy your neighbours. Caravans and awnings are scarcely soundproof, and noise carries far at night. You should never allow your music, merrymaking, dogs or children to annoy other people. This is one of the basic principles of the Caravan Code. Silence at night is a matter which is strictly observed, particularly on continental sites.

Tool Kit

Always carry a tool kit, but don't go berserk since weight quickly adds up here. We always carry a hammer *(for awning pegs)*, a medium and small blade screwdriver plus the same size Phillips screwdrivers, a hand drill and bits, some fine emery paper for electric contacts, pliers, wire strippers, spare lengths of wire, plus of course, suitable fuses. Also take insulating tape *(good for water pipes or car hoses in emergencies)*, a Stanley knife, miniature hacksaw, a few screws and fastenings, plus self-tapping screws, a spirit level and tape measure, a can of WD40 lubricating spray, a small pot of grease, a few rubber bands, a tube of Evo-stik and some strong twine. In addition to these, we carry a tow rope and a set of jump leads. A torque wrench and jack for the van are always carried. We have rarely needed any of this equipment, but are sure we would have done if we hadn't actually had it with us.

Sometimes in the timeless tranquillity of a summer holiday, and armed with these items, I will take some vital part of the caravan to pieces and then reassemble it again - just for the hell of it. This is a pastime which Herself views with a disappointing lack of confidence, but at least it keeps me out of the pubs.

Portable Larder

Another useful piece of kit is a camping larder. This is virtually an oblong box, about 2½ feet high, 18 inches wide and about 12 inches deep. It is made of lightweight nylon fabric with net panels for ventilation and has three hardboard shelves. It folds down completely flat for stowage and weighs very little. In use, it hangs from nylon strings with an 'S' hook at the top, and we hang it in the awning. It will accommodate a fair quantity of salad stuff, fruit and vegetables; all things which are not heavy but take up a lot of cupboard space in the van, and which are better stored out in the fresh air. It has a zip fastening and is completely insect proof. It is available in most camping shops.

Equipment List

Keep a notebook with a checklist of everything you need to take with you, and I mean everything. Don't classify anything as being so obvious that only a half-wit would forget to pack it. More than one seasoned caravanner has got halfway to Dover before a casual query from the better half has established that the spare wheel/suitcase/passports/loo are still at home on the driveway.

It could be advantageous for one person to be specifically responsible for the list, which should include absolutely everything that isn't actually screwed down in the caravan. Sewing kit, torch, tools, awning, cooking gear, bedding, fly swat - if it's needed, great or small, it should be in the book. Only when you have been finely honed on the stone of bitter experience will you have compiled a list that includes everything you really need to take.

By this time, however, you will find you are severely overweight so you must start to edit your list. *(If things go as they normally do, you will then find that you won't use half the things you take, and that you have urgent need of bits you left at home. All this, of course, adds to the bitter-sweet charm of the sport.)*

It is well worth thoroughly checking your list, even though it takes time to compile. It's no good, for example saying 'we must bring a left-handed corkscrew next time' and promptly forgetting about it - put it on the list there and then.

The Caravan Club have a checklist with extra space for you to add your own special items, as do many caravan dealers.

Carpet Protection

A thought about your caravan carpet, if fitted, with the inevitable spillages of food etc, which are almost impossible to avoid, it does tend to bear the brunt of stains in the catering area. The answer is a length of clear, heavy plastic carpet protector. This comes in a roll 27 inches wide and can be obtained from most accessory shops.

Only with bitter sweet experience will you have a complete list of all things needed

10

The trouble is that it 'walks' along the pile of the carpet, and should be secured as follows. Fix a short length of half-an-inch wide strong tape, or a strip of the clear plastic itself, at right angles to the edge of the plastic in three places, one towards each end and one in the centre. The tapes (or strips) should project about one inch beyond the edge of the plastic and finish with a small brass 'D' ring. Fasten the tape to the top of the plastic protecting strip, through the 'D' ring, and fold it back on itself to fasten underneath the strip. The tapes can be fastened to the plastic with either Evo-stik or pop-rivets plus washers, or better still, both. The 'D' rings then hook on to three small brass cuphooks fixed just above floor level at suitable intervals along the base of the kitchen unit. There is usually a stiffening batten running along the inside of the unit, and this will accept the cuphooks.

Accidents will inevitably happen so protection is necessary

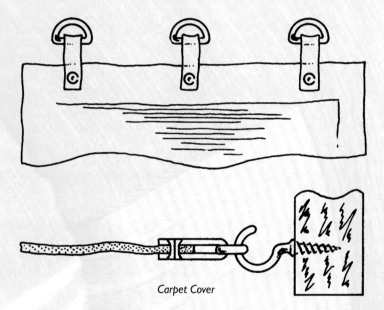

Carpet Cover

The plastic can be sponged or scrubbed easily and will certainly preserve your carpet in this rather vulnerable area.

While I was actually working on the update for an earlier edition of the book, the value of this plastic carpet protector was vividly illustrated. We were holed-up on a certificated location amid magnificent scenery in the Lake District. It was the Happy Hour. Wine had been poured and Herself was assembling a succulent omelette - mushrooms, tomatoes, onions, garlic, the whole works. The aroma in the confines of the caravan was at once tantalising and full of promise. At the crucial moment, armed with a spatula thing, Herself went to transfer the creation from pan to plate, and missed.

'Never mind,' you are thinking, 'at least it would fall on this much acclaimed piece of plastic.'

Alas no.

She missed that as well and once again waxed eloquent. Still, it's an ill wind; the dog thought it was her birthday, and we ate a little later, What we need now is either a bigger piece of carpet protector or bigger plates.

Caravan step

With the corner steadies wound down, taking some of the caravan's weight at each corner, the height from ground level up to the floor of the van can be around 18 inches. This is too great a height to be mounted comfortably in one go, so some form of step is needed.

Most steps are either of rigid plastic or tubular metal construction with a non-slip rubber surface on the top, and are designed to combine strength with minimum weight.

A one-tread step is sometimes difficult for a child or a handicapped person, so a two tier step is available which effectively divides the climb into three stages, instead of the two-stage effect of a single step and these are much more stable.

Most accessory shops offer a good choice of caravan steps, including these described above. PLUS an additional most useful and sensible piece of kit

We mentioned a tool kit a couple of pages back, but where are we going to store these screwdrivers, pliers and whatnots? The answer is in a toolbox-cum-caravan step. This is a particularly sturdy plastic box of similar dimensions to a step. It has a reinforced hinged lid and a removable tray inside, a recessed carrying handle and a lockable hasp. This is one of these two in one gadgets that really does have a practical application. It certainly does hold a surprising amount of odds and ends that normally tend to clutter up drawers inside the caravan. Highly recommended.

Jacking Systems

Punctures on a caravan are thankfully rare. In all our years of caravanning I think we've only had one. It was on a narrowish, downhill, winding road in Somerset, with a double white line down the centre, and the puncture was, of course, in the offside wheel. I remember it vividly.

> Punctures on a caravan are thankfully rare

10

We put our red triangle out further up the road, and Herself gallantly directed traffic around me as I knelt in the road, my backside sticking out, laboriously jacking up the laden caravan.

When a scissors jack is wound right down, the lack of mechanical advantage makes winding up a very heavy task indeed. A hydraulic or 'bottle' jack is often too tall to get under the axle, or chassis member, and both of these are difficult to access in the confines of a caravan wheel arch. The ideal solution is a small trolley jack, but the sheer weight of this makes it impractical to cart about as part of your standard in-van equipment.

I carry a small hydraulic 'bottle' jack. It's usually the simplest way to raise the van with a minimum of effort. Trouble is, if you have a flat tyre, the chassis is going to be even nearer the ground, and you won't have room to get the jack under the axle or the chassis.

Towing on to blocks

Remember the pieces of wood we referred to in **Chapter 2** - unhitching and levelling? *(Illustration repeated above)*. Place these chunks of wood in front of the punctured wheel and carefully tow the caravan up onto the wood, and this should give you enough clearance to get the jack underneath.

An alternative piece of kit is the Al-Ko side lift jack designed for use with Al-Ko chassis. This is stocked by most caravan dealers' accessory shops. Cost is in the region of £65. Al-Ko have recently added an up-rated version of the side lift jack to cope with a twin axle caravan. Retail about £80.00 - **See Useful Contacts**.

Checklist:

General Hints

1 Brighten an old caravan with new curtains/ loose covers. ✓

2 Mosquito nets are a must in Europe (and in Scotland!). ✓

3 Never block up ventilators. ✓

4 Check tyres and wheel nuts. ✓

5 Do carry a spare wheel, plus jack and wheel brace. ✓

6 Avoid parking directly under trees. ✓

7 Install a car cassette/radio or CD player - better than a portable one. ✓

8 Carry a tool kit. ✓

9 Keep a notebook or checklist of things to pack.

SAS PRODUCTS
1987-2010
Keeping you safe & secure for 23 years

SAS SUPACLAMP for Alloy wheels
◆ FITS ALL CARAVAN ALLOY WHEELS 10-15" RIMS, UP TO 195 SIZES TYRES
◆ COVERS A WHEEL NUT and LOCKS SECURELY
◆ AROUND THE WHEEL
◆ SUPERBLY STRONG
◆ TWIN LOCKING MECHANISM for MAXIMUM SECURITY
◆ FITS IN SECONDS-IDEAL for STORAGE or TOURING
◆ SUPPLIED in RED CARRY CASE
◆ **SOLD SECURE and INSURANCE APPROVED**

FORT2GOLD HITCHLOCK
◆ FITS ALKO STABILISING HITCHES
◆ AKS1300,2004,3004 AS WELL AS STANDARD ALKO HITCH HEADS
◆ FITS HITCHED and UNHITCHED.
◆ SUPPLIED in PREMIUM ALUMINIUM CARRY CASE.
◆ **SOLD SECURE and INSURANCE APPROVED**

SOLD SECURE
TESTED TO
REDUCE CRIME

OUR SUPERB CORNER STEADY LOCKS CONTINUE TO PROTECT YOUR CARAVAN FROM THEFT
TWIN PACK- *Locks 2 steadies in down position*
FOUR PACK-*Locks 4 steadies in down position*
(either supplied keyed alike)

NARCOTIC GAS ALARM

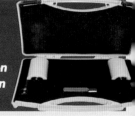

◆ THIS 12V/24V GAS ALARM DETECTS ALL NARCOTIC GASES AS WELL AS BUTANE, PROPANE, METHANE, ETHANOL, LPG and OTHER COMBUSTIBLE GASSES.
◆ IT HAS BUILT IN BACK UP 9V BATTERY-SO IF YOUR 12/24V BATTERY SUPPLY FAILS or IS DELIBERATELY CUT THE ALARM SYSTEM WILL ACTIVATE IMMEDIATELY
◆ THIS EFFECTIVE GAS ALARM OFFERS YOU MAXIMUM PROTECTION FROM GAS ATTACKS or GAS LEAKS WHEN IN YOUR CARAVAN/MOTORHOME/TRUCK AT ALL TIMES.

www.sasproducts.com   email:sales@sasproducts.com   Tel: 0117 937 474

Security

Looking back it seems that, with each edition of this book, the chapter on security gets longer. I'm afraid it reflects the times in which we live. When we first caravanned, we could go out for the day and leave all the windows open. Alas, not now. Caravans disappear from people's gardens, from secure, locked compounds, from caravan sites and from motorway service stations. One result is a growing proliferation of security devices, varying from excellent down to near-useless.

Some accessory manufacturers tend to jump on the bandwagon in marketing gimmicks on the basis that anything to do with security will sell. It usually pays, however, to deal with security specialists.

Such a company is Safe And Secure Products *(SAS)* of Bristol. As their name suggests, caravan security is their principal concern and so this chapter sees their products referred to frequently.

The problem for the caravanner is twofold: first to prevent his van being taken away in the first place, and second to be able to positively identify it if and when it is recovered or recognised as a stolen caravan.

The good news, however, is that through the use of effective security devices combined with efficient caravan identification schemes, caravan thefts can be contained and are slowly decreasing. We look at such an identification scheme later in this chapter.

> A caravan can be stolen in less than a minute

Immobilisation

The first problem is dealt with by making the caravan immobile on site. Originally this was dealt with simply by fitting a hitch lock. Locks are available to fit most types of coupling head, making it difficult to attach the caravan to a towing vehicle. However, determined caravan thieves will, if necessary, unbolt the entire coupling and jockey wheel housing from the 'A' frame, and fit another. All the caravan owner is then left with is his coupling head unit, complete with hitch lock still attached. Practised thieves have more than once stolen a hitch-locked caravan by fastening the coupling head *(and hitch lock)* to the getaway vehicle with rope, and removing the hitch lock at their leisure.

However, hitch locks are a deterrent and will often prevent the spur of the moment theft where the thieves do not have time on their side.

For example, caravan thefts from motorway service area car parks are by no means uncommon - it takes about 45 seconds for your caravan to be unhitched from your car, dropped onto the towball of the getaway vehicle and driven away. If you do make a stop at such a location it is really worth just dropping your jockey wheel, unhitching your van, applying the handbrake and fixing a hitch lock. It only takes a minute or so.

SAS market a particularly secure hitch lock called 'Fortress' which has a maximum security safe type lock with twin locking mechanisms and anti-drill protection. It can be used with the caravan unhitched, hitched and locked to the car, or locked to a security post and costs £49.99.

In addition to the older type of open handle coupling heads, SAS also supply hitch locks for Al-Ko style stabilising couplings. This is the Fortress 2, retailing at around £70.

A neat alternative to the lock-it-all-in-box type of hitch lock is a new SAS security product called the Rock Lock. This is a tough security bolt which fits through the coupling head, and prevents release. Like the 'Fortress', it can be used with the caravan hitched or unhitched *(but shold not be used whilst towing)*.

Ensure your caravan is still there when you get back from the beach

It is small, lightweight and very reasonably priced at around £25. It can also be used with a loop chain made of hardened steel with a double fabric sleeve to prevent scratching. It then has an inner narrow width of chain links - all resistant to attacks. The Rock Lock with chain retails at £49.99.

A phone call to their Bristol office will bring detailed leaflets on any of the SAS products described in this section, or a general leaflet detailing the entire range of caravan security products. **See** *Useful Contacts* **at the back of the book**

Most caravan accessory shops stock a wide range of caravan security devices, including many from the SAS range.

Once established on a site, there are a number of precautions you can take to ensure that your caravan is still there when you get back from the beach and these usually take the form of either hitch locks, wheel clamps, internal intruder alarms, or a permutation of all three. An additional deterrent to the thief is to fit one or more leg locks to your corner steadies. Available for corner steady legs, either with or without guide tubes. Pictured is the HDLL, around £19.95.

Wheel clamps take various forms and more recent designs are now proving an effective deterrent. SAS market wheelclamps for both steel and alloy wheels which, on testing, have achieved the highest security grading of 'Sold Secure'. The latest of these is the Gridlock, designed to fit 2006 and later caravans with alloy wheels, which have the Al-Ko Lock Receiver fitted behind the wheels. Lock Receivers are available from SAS. Gridlock type clamps are so effective that they attract premium discounts from some insurers. Single axle versions cost around £150 and twin axle £199. Not cheap, you might say, but probably no more than 1% of the replacement cost of your caravan. Better Safe than Sorry.

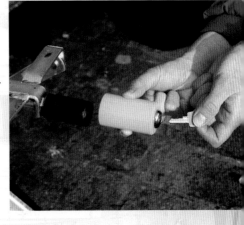

A really muscular wheel clamp in the SAS range is the New Defender, it's as tough as its name suggests. Now in two sizes, it covers up to 18″ wheels and 275mm tyres or up to 22″ wheels and 295mm. tyres.

It is easily adjustable and completely covers the wheel nuts, with no need to remove the wheel trim. The hardened lock is drill-proof and pick-proof, and deflating the tyre has no effect on its rigid fixing. The centre area of the clamp is coloured a bright red, giving clear warning of a substantial security device. It is specifically designed to fit inside restricted wheel arches.

Wheel clamps come in all shapes and sizes

Rugged it may be, but clumsy it is not. Careful design has ensured very easy fitting, comfortable carrying and compact folding for storage.

When I first inspected it I had two immediate reactions. The first was that here was a wheel clamp that will definitely not

surrender to bolt cutters or hacksaws. The second thought was its weight. It is really thief resistant and tough, and the gauge of metal required to produce this is necessarily heavy. If you are critical on towing weight you may need to think carefully before taking the New Defender on holiday. For securing your caravan at home or in storage, however, this is the one. My impression was that if some cowboy takes your van with the New Defender in place, he'll probably have to leave the axle behind.

A rigged awning, incidentally, is no deterrent to the quick removal of a caravan. A sharp knife run around the awning close to its joint with the van, and your awning is removed *(and totally ruined)* in seconds.

Another effective piece of kit by SAS is a heavy-duty hardened steel post, the socket for which can be concreted into the ground, the two units being joined by an armour-plated anti-tamper padlock which is protected against bolt cutters. If the caravan is stored in the right angle between two walls, a single post will form an impassable barrier to the removal of the van. The tow hitch of the caravan may be locked onto the 50mm ball at the top of the post, and secured by an SAS heavy-duty hitch lock. The post is resistant to ramming. A range of security posts in various sizes is available.

Wheelclamps come in different forms but it is a fact that real gutsy, he-man clamps are made from the quality and gauge of steel favoured by the Royal Tank Regiment. On top of this they need a considerable area of steel plate to protect the central area of the wheel in order to guard against the removal of the wheel itself, all of which makes for a weighty piece of equipment. We have agreed that, excellent deterrents though they are, clamps of this sort are best used at home and/or for winter storage. They are too bulky and heavy to cart about on holidays.

A much needed device from SAS is the 'Supaclamp Gold' which has been specifically designed for alloy wheels - now increasingly in use on up-market caravans.

The Supaclamp, unlike others, avoids damaging contact with the wheel rim, but locks over the wheelnut. It has twin locking mechanism and is easily attached. Ideal for touring, it retails at about £89.99.

Consider the weight when choosing wheelclamps

In addition to good quality locking wheel studs, SAS market a very effective dummy wheel for winter storage called the Winter Wheels Gold with "Sold Secure" status. The photograph shows this with wheel studs visible. A sturdy steel plate then locks over the front, covering the wheel studs. Two stands, two locking plates and two locking wheel bolts retail at £105. Available in either 4 or 5 stud fittings, the Winter Wheel Gold is good value.

There are effective ways to safeguard the contents too

Locks and Alarms

So much for not losing the caravan. What about its contents? It is not necessary to get inside a van to steal it, as the thieves can always get inside once they have removed it from your location. The security of its contents on site is a different matter, however.

Additional door security can be provided by fitting a modified cylinder to the existing caravan door lock. These are available quite reasonably from Safe and Secure Products. There are over 50,000 different combinations of keys to these easily fitted cylinders - well worth installing.

Such a modification won't keep out anyone who sets about the lower half of the door with a lever or jemmy, but you can deter this character by fitting to the lower door a sturdy deadlock which actually bolts through into the door frame when locked.

This leaves the windows, which usually have several fastenings each. When leaving the caravan unattended, do fasten all windows properly. This will deter the opportunist thief, but you cannot keep out one who is really determined to get in. At the expense of smashing the fastenings and probably the window itself, anyone with a jemmy or similar tool can open a caravan window and, working on the window inside an awning, would be unobserved even on a busy site.

In this case you must consider some sort of electronic burglar alarm with a noise warning. Beware of anything too sensitive, such as those designed to detect movement. A window trembler switch is easily set off just by the wind gently rocking the caravan.

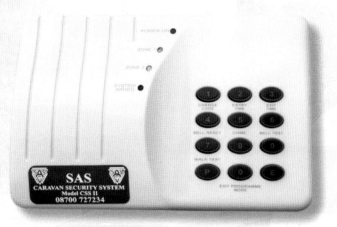

SAS have now superseded their original security alarm with Caravan Security System II. This features a passive infra-red motion detector sensor to detect any intruder, plus a tilt motion detector and corner steady vibration sensor. In addition, there are magnetic window and door contacts, and all these devices are connected to a horrendously loud waterproof external siren.

The system incorporates a simple control panel which allows you to select your own 4-digit entry code, siren time plus entry/exit time. 12-volt connection is supplied, plus a back-up power supply. The whole system sells for £99.99, and is an effective safeguard against theft.

They also market another security item which certainly deserves a mention. An ingenious idea, it consists of a range of cans such as may be found in any kitchen cupboard; beer cans, Coca-Cola, and various household names, all authentically lettered, they just look like commonplace items. However the bottom unscrews to provide a far from obvious hiding place for money, watches, jewellery etc. The containers are suitably weighted to feel authentic if picked up and they constitute a much cheaper alternative to an underfloor safe.

Hitch locks, lockable corner steadies, dummy wheel plates and various types of burglar alarm are all well advertised in specialist caravan magazines and, of course, caravan dealers can offer both equipment and advice,

It is not my intention to deter you with this dismal survey of possibilities. Thankfully, in over 40 years, we have never had anything stolen. Caravans are ransacked however, and taken by theft. The moral is: do take reasonable precautions and don't cut corners with questionable insurance cover. Get your caravan and all its contents, including money, cameras etc, fully covered. We'll talk about insurance a few pages further on.

Tracking Devices

If, despite all the precautionary gear described in this chapter, your caravan is stolen, your chances of recovering it are vastly increased if it is fitted with a tracking device.

Global Positioning technology has enabled SAS to market some pretty slick equipment which works in conjunction with your mobile phone.

The TRACK & TEXT unit is a compact 8 cms x 10 cms, which can be concealed in the bottom of the wardrobe, in a bed locker or wherever. Powered by a small 12 volt lead-acid battery, it bas a 6v back up battery, and Track & Text will text your mobile when the main battery runs out.

Hi-Tech available for the security of your caravan

The caravan will text you if it is moved, broken into or suffers fire, smoke or flood, and you can provide the unit with up to 20 mobile phone numbers to alert.

If moved, the Track & Text will advise latitude and longitude via global satellite in plain English at a cost of £1 per location text.

The Track & Text unit costs around £600, so you would not fit it into a 30 year old £850 caravan, but alas, the majority of valuable stolen caravans are never traced, so it is something well worth consideration. This is a reasonable price for such sophisticated technology.

In the field of caravan security SAS are pretty well in pole position, but they don't stop there. In addition to the more widely known security gear, they stock items like ground anchors, heavy duty barrier and security posts, anchorages for motorbiles, builders' plant etc., a wide range of virtually impregnable padlocks, chains, and garage door security. They also market a range of walkie-talkie pocket radios with ranges up to five kilometres. For a look at their extensive range of security equipment **visit their website at** www.sasproducts.com

Of course, SAS are not the only people in their field. Equally good quality security equipment is marketed by Bulldog Security Products and stocked by a wide range of caravan dealers accessory shops. *Ring **Bulldog** on 01952 728171.*

A trade directory of firms who market caravan security equipment in one form or another actually lists 96 different suppliers, and it is not the purpose of this volume to list them. I have described the sort of equipment you might need, dear reader, and identified two excellent sources; the rest is up to you. Just do be aware that we sadly live in a wicked world, where stuff gets nicked. You need to insure against this and be aware of the fact that unless you take reasonable precautions to safeguard your property, the insureres won't pay up if it's stolen.

Caravan Registration and Identification Scheme (CRiS)

The National Caravan Council launched, in 1992, the CRiS scheme in cooperation with all UK manufacturers who were NCC members. Since 1992 all UK manufactured caravans have had a Vehicle Identity Number *(VIN)* unique to the van. The coded number identifies the individual van, and the manufacturer among other details; it is clearly etched on every window and die stamped on the chassis. Since 1997, the number has also been on a microchip hidden somewhere on board.

VIN's - an effective means to identify your caravan

Every new caravan has a registration document bearing the VIN, and the new owner completes his details on the appropriate section and returns it to the CRiS office for computerised registration. On a change of ownership, the new owner can verify the caravan's details, and both vendor and purchaser fill in the relevant parts of the document and return to CRiS. It is similar to the detailed register of motor vehicles maintained by the DVLA. There is a £10 fee payable on registering a change of ownership.

Since 1997 it has been possible to register a pre-1992 or an imported caravan with CRiS, for which a fee of £37.12 is payable *(What is the 12p for? I don't know, and nobody else seems to know)*. Anyway, there is a £5 discount for members of either of the two main clubs, and the fee includes a kit for etching the allotted CRiS number on the windows and an electronic coded tag device for secreting somewhere on the caravan.

They also operate the Towsafe service for safe matching of cars and caravans, which we described in *Chapter 1*. It is the same phone number for both services, ie *01722 411430*.

The scheme is operated for the National Caravan Council by HPI, who have extensive experience of monitoring and processing vehicle related data. *Telephone 01722 411430* **for details.**

The scheme must now be the biggest national database of touring caravans, and makes the illegal sale of stolen ones considerably more difficult.

Insurance

This section on caravan insurance is an important part of the whole subject of security.

As with household, car, personal or any other type of insurance cover, it is wise to get several quotes, look at the small print and thoroughly understand what you are getting for your money. It does not follow that the cheapest cover is the best buy, nor for that matter, that the most expensive is necessarily the best cover.

Many insurance companies and brokers will quote you for insurance cover on your caravan, but in this area it is probably sensible to deal with a specialist company.

One example is Mobile Homes Insurance Service of Leamington Spa **See** *Useful Contacts* **at the back of the book**. I have dealt with them for several years and found them efficient and competitive.

Most caravan dealers hold an agency for an insurance company, but not all are necessarily good value.

Each of the two major caravan clubs has its own policy for members, and mention of their respective insurance services is made in Chapter 8.

Both clubs offer comprehensive forms of cover against the various caravan related disasters to which we are all exposed. The Camping and Caravanning Club can quote favourable rates for insurance cover on caravans, cars, motor caravans and houses. Full details are available from the Camping and Caravanning Club. **See** *Useful Contacts* **at the back of the book**

The Caravan Club maintains a register of members' caravans by make, chassis number etc. This is an important feature of the Club's service, and of course they offer practical forms of caravan insurance, the premiums varying with the value insured and the extent of the cover required. The Club can also quote for car, motor caravan and house insurance, as do the Camping and Caravanning Club. Two additional services offered by both Clubs are a pet care policy and insurance for small craft - sailing dinghies and similar craft.

It is important to realise that no insurance company will pay out on a claim for theft or similar loss unless the policy-holder has taken reasonable care of the property. Leaving a caravan unattended and unlocked, or with windows unfastened, or indeed without some form of anti-theft device on the van itself, would almost certainly be considered negligence on the part of the insured.

Compare quotes and read the small print

On the subject of small print, a cautionary tale came to light recently which should serve as a warning to all.

A gentleman had his caravan insured with a company who offered a discount on premiums, on condition that a wheel clamp was fixed whenever the van was not being towed. With his van laid up for the winter in a locked compound, the caravanner decided to go one better and removed both wheels. When the thieves came for his caravan they brought their own wheels and the van disappeared. The insurers refused to pay up because a wheel clamp was not in use.

This smacks of Alice in Wonderland to me and the insurers seem to be dodging their contractual obligations on fairly thin grounds. Their case was that the caravanner had abandoned his contractual obligations by not having a wheel clamp in use, an undertaking he had previously given in order to qualify for a reduced premium. So, the moral is do read the small print. Know exactly what you're getting for your premium, and what your obligations in the contract amount to.

Since this incident occurred I believe insurers have waived this requirement for a fitted wheel clamp when both wheels are removed, and a final word here on removing wheels for winter storage seems appropriate.

About the simplest domestic building to break into is the average garage - double doors, up and over, or whatever. If you store your caravan for the winter at home, and remove the wheels in the process, don't store the wheels in the garage. It's the first place they will look, and don't forget the third wheel, the caravan spare. Take them upstairs and stash them in the loft. It is preferable to achieve this when Head Office has gone shopping, or you will be stood over, complete with damp cloth, dustpan and brush. Tyre marks on the wallpaper make for very few brownie points.

Apart from the two clubs, I would also single out Shield Insurance, who offer many different types of cover, but tend to specialise in caravan and motor home insurance. **See** *Useful Contacts* **at the back of the book**. They are part of IGI Insurance, who initiated an ever growing network of secure caravan storage sites around the UK, which leads us neatly on to the last section in this security chapter.

Safe Storage

Finally, where is the safest place to store your caravan when you're not using it?

At home in the driveway, alongside the garage or whatever, is certainly the most convenient, although many houses are built on land which carries a covenant prohibiting the siting of caravans in

The average domestic garage is the easiest building to break into. Store the wheels else where

this manner. We have reviewed a range of security devices in this chapter, but often little more than a wheel clamp and a hitch lock are used at home and it is worth noting that around 40% of stolen vans have been lifted from people's drives and front gardens.

Many farmers will offer storage in barns, but such sites are soon known to thieves and are not particularly secure. No, the answer lies in some sort of purpose built compound.

Sadly, the lawless times in which we live have prompted IGI Insurance to set up a non-profit making organisation called the Caravan Storage Site Owners Association *(CaSSOA)*. Members of CaSSOA have premises where a high degree of security is assured, secure fencing, only one entrance with secure access, floodlighting, and a high degree of presence on site are some of the features.

Storage at such sites can reduce insurance premiums, but an insurer will often check the degree of security in place with the actual site owner.

Insurer's stipulations tend to vary, some do actually work on the principle that storage on the owner's own premises is preferable, so if you have a choice of storage options, you will need to shop around.

Obviously with dedicated secure storage sites, the price will vary according to the degree of security offered.

Details and locations of participating sites, many of which are on farms, can be had either by a phone call to their Nottingham office, or a visit to their website **See** *Useful Contacts* **at the back of the book**.

Dedicated secure storage sites could be the best option

Security

1 Security precautions: two aims – prevent loss of entire caravan, and prevent entry and loss of contents. ✓

2 Preventing forced entry is virtually impossible but deterrents are well worthwhile. ✓

3 Preventing theft of the van means immobilising it by one, preferably more, means. ✓

4 Immobilisation is essential during storage or lay-up. ✓

5 Etch your chassis number or postcode on caravan windows, if not already done. ✓

6 Similarly, mark interior surfaces with invisible (ultraviolet) pen. ✓

7 Register your van's identity with the Caravan Club. ✓

8 A record of all stolen vans is maintained by the National Caravan Council. ✓

9 Take out a fully comprehensive insurance policy. ✓

10 Lock your caravan and car whenever you leave them, even for brief absences. Your insurance will not cover you if you have not taken reasonable care. ✓

11 If your caravan is CRiS registered, don't keep the registration and identification document in the van. ✓

12 Consider a hidden microchip identity scheme, or tag, if not already fitted. ✓

13 Read the small print on your insurance policy. ✓

Maintenance and Laying Up

Most caravanners use their van from the spring through until autumn, then lay it up for the winter, although year-round and 'frostbite' caravanning is becoming increasingly popular.

Many of the small jobs listed here can be done prior to laying up, or on recommissioning in the spring, or preferably check over on both occasions. Obviously a caravan is better stored under cover, bearing in mind that wet and damp are the main enemies. If under cover, however, adequate ventilation is essential. A caravan, like a car, will suffer more harm than good if it is shut in an unventilated, damp garage.

It should be strongly emphasised that the periodic checks made under the various headings in this chapter are NOT a substitute for a thorough professional workshops service, which should be carried out annually.

Although most caravan dealers' workshops are qualified to do this, the following section gives details of the nationwide network of workshops who are members of the Approved Caravan Workshop scheme.

An annual thorough professional service is essential

Annual Service and Electricity Check

The NCC, Caravan Club, and Camping and Caravanning Club recommend that all caravans are serviced annually. Therefore the NCC, Caravan Club and the Automobile Association launched the Approved Caravan Workshop programme at the 1996 Caravan Show held at Earls Court.

The service centres had to abide by a code of practice and a detailed service schedule drawn up by the Approval Board. The Approval Board included a representative from each of the three organisations involved in the programme.

The AA engineers undertook unannounced checks twice a year at each approved workshop to ensure they were continuing to comply with the requirements of the scheme.

In 1998 the AA withdrew from the scheme, however, and the Camping and Caravanning Club joined the Caravan Club and the National Caravan Council as a member of the organising body, and Jones Vening were recruited to take care of the

12

technical side. They are responsible for the uniformity of service schedules carried out by all workshops and for the careful maintenance of standards. At the time of writing there are over 180 dealers' workshops who participate in the scheme and the number is rising.

The Jones Vening website will give you all necessary information, plus a list of approved workshops throughout the UK. **Visit www.jones-vening.co.uk, or call them on 01547 560456.**

If your caravan is fitted with mains electricity remember that the system should be checked professionally at least every 3 years, and a new 16th Edition IEE Wiring Regulations periodic inspection report issued.

My brother has lived in Cornwall for many years and recently mentioned to one of his buddies that he was taking his car in for a service.

Regular servicing can save money - and the risk factor

"What's wrong with it?" asked the native of Cornshire.

"Nothing" said my brother.

"Well why are you having it serviced then?" was the reply.

This philosophy is by no means restricted to the West Country. "If it ain't broke, don't fix it" certainly does NOT apply to caravans.

This is a policy which, in the long run, costs more money than it saves, and without doubt it puts the occupants AND the public at risk. We saw in the water supply section how failure to renew water filters has prompted some caravan manufacturers to stop fitting them altogether.

I cannot emphasise too strongly the very real need to have a caravan professionally serviced at least one a year.

This should cover the gas system, 12-volt and mains electrics, brakes, chassis, suspension, wheel bearings, coupling head, jockey wheel, road lights, hob and oven, taps and micro-switches, smoke alarm, a damp check on the caravan body plus the operation of the fridge, water heater and space heater.

Tyres

Starting at the bottom: check your tyres for damage - if you can jack up your van so that the wheels are off the ground, so much the better. Support the suspension or chassis on axle stands - don't let the weight rest solely on the corner steadies; they are not designed for this. If you cannot raise the wheels, then occasionally jack up, and partly rotate each wheel, so that the tyres are not constantly flexed in one position. The wheels would be better off removed from the caravan during the winter and stored well away from the caravan *(not in the garage)* for two reasons. One, the tyres will benefit from not being flexed in one position; and two it is harder to steal a caravan without wheels, though by no means impossible.

Another, timely warning on tyres comes from the British Rubber Manufacturers Association *(BRMA)*. It appears that some older caravans with wheels designed for tyres with inner tubes have been fitted with tubeless tyres. This is a potentially dangerous situation which can lead to the deflation of tyres on cornering and even to the complete loss of the tyre from the wheel. The BRMA advise that wheels designed for tubed tyres should never be fitted with tubeless tyres and wheels designed for tubeless tyres should never be fitted with inner tubes.

Owners of older vans may well be unaware of the actions of a previous owner with regard to replacement tyres, so after buying an older caravan, owners are strongly advised to get the wheels and tyres carefully checked at a specialist tyre depot.

When a replacement tyre is wanted for a caravan, be it for the spare or straight on to the axle, one does not usually take the caravan to the tyre depot, just the wheel. It is all too common on these occasions for the owner to ask for a cheap tyre to be fitted, without mentioning that it is to go on a caravan. Whether it is a remould or a low-grade tyre is not thought important. 'It will have a decent tread on it and that's what matters.' WRONG!

There is far more to a tyre than just a good tread. For a start, on a single axle caravan - and this is the vast majority - each wheel is bearing about twice the load that each of the four tyres carries on an average car.

You should always specify that the tyre is for a caravan and the depot should, if they are doing their job, fit a 6-ply or a reinforced tyre. If you examine a new tyre carefully you will see on the tyre wall a whole jumble of letters and codes, which almost need a separate handbook to interpret. You should find, however, the maximum load that the tyre is designed to carry and the maximum speed at which that load can be carried. A 4-ply tyre, a remould or any sort of 'bargain' tyre will certainly not come up to the specification you need.

Apart from being a security measure, removing the van wheels in winter will help preserve your tyres. An inflated tyre has its walls stretched, that much is obvious. In cold weather with the tyre constantly flexed in one position, hairline cracks or 'crazing' will take place on the walls and, to a lesser extent, even with the wheels jacked up. Better to remove the wheels completely.

You should always specify if a tyre is for a caravan

Chassis

If you do not have a modern galvanised chassis *(pre-1980 caravans)* so unlikely now, check for rust - any rust spots should be cleaned with a stiff wire brush and treated with a rust inhibitor. Halfords offer a variety of these. Paint over the area with black bitumastic paint, or better still use Finnegan's Hammerite in black.

If any part of the chassis, suspension or brake mechanism shows signs of rust, treat as above then spray the whole lot with Finnegan's Waxoyl. *(Again this is available from Halfords, and includes a hand spray applicator.)* Waxoyl will inhibit rust, lubricate and form a hard wax seal against further damp. Care must be taken not to spray it on polystyrene sheeting which at one time was used as under-floor insulation. A chemical in Waxoyl will dissolve polystyrene, but is not harmful to wood or tyres.

Floors

Check the caravan floor for a springy or spongey feeling when walked on. If this occurs, you probably have delamination taking place.

For over 25 years caravan floors have consisted of a bonded sandwich; two fairly thin sheets of plywood with a thicker sheet of polystyrene foam in between and all glued together under pressure. Neither of these materials has much strength individually, but the composite sandwich is very strong indeed.

However, if these individual sheets come unglued, the strength of the floor - on which the chassis relies - is greatly weakened, and the spongey feeling is a warning symptom.

A caravan dealer's workshop can fix this by injecting a special glue and reapplying the bonding pressure.

Don't disregard a delaminating floor, the ultimate cure will be expensive indeed.

Watch out for gas - check for gas leaks

Gas and Water Pipes

While underneath, check gas and water pipes. Joints in gas pipes can be checked for leaks as follows. Turn on the gas at the relevant cylinder, ensuring that the gas taps at all appliances are in the off position. Brush a soap or detergent solution over the joints in the supply line. Any sign of bubbles will indicate a leak, and the gentle tightening of the nut with a spanner should effect a cure. If not, undo the nut from the joint and replace the olive. The olive is a soft metal collar which fits around the supply pipe, and the action of tightening the nut will compress the olive against a recess in the joint, forming a gas-tight seal.

Gas pipe joints and olives are obtainable from dealers but make sure you get the correct size since more than one diameter of pipe is used on a supply system.

Fresh water pipes should be free of algae or blobs of discolouration. If the pipes don't appear to be clean, pump a purifying solution through the whole system and allow it to stand for a few hours before flushing through with clean water. Middle aged caravans are fitted with coloured rather then clear water pipes - black or blue for cold water, red for hot. This is largely because algae forms more readily in clear pipes. If you have an old caravan with clear plastic piping, replace it with coloured piping. If you are doing some DIY plumbing, do use special red pipe for hot water, it is designed for the job.

It is worth noting that from about 1999, caravan manufacturers started using semi-rigid 12mm plastic pipes for internal water systems. These have simple push fit joints, including right-angled elbows, which avoid the problems experienced with flexible plastic pipe when bent through 90 degrees. This causes kinking, and inevitably reduces flow.

You can obtain sterilising tablets from accessory shops, or a preparation of sodium metabisulphite which is available from Boots or any winemaking shop (it is used extensively to sterilise wine and beer making equipment). Check all water pipe joints for leaks, tightening up the jubilee clips if necessary. Before doing so, give the jubilee clip screws a squirt of WD40 lubricant.

A modern or 'winterised' caravan will probably not have gas or water pipes visible from the underside. These will all be routed through the interior of the van, passing through the dividing walls of cupboards, bedding lockers etc.

This makes for higher building costs, but lessens the likelihood of freezing up in winter. The cleaning of water pipes can still be carried out as described above, and at your annual service, your caravan dealer's workshops will always carry out a leakage check on your entire gas supply system. In the interests of safety this should be done at least once a year.

Waste water pipes, ie those draining water from shower tray, wash basin and kitchen sink should also be sterilised. They often consist of flexible corrugated ¾" plastic pipe in which waste water and bits of food can lie trapped, and these become a health hazard and a source of unpleasant smells.

Clean these by corking up the end of the outlet pipes outside the van, and allow a strong solution of sterilising fluid or disinfectant to stand in the pipes for an hour or so.

> Avoid health hazards by sterilising the pipes

Grease and Lubricate

Take a grease gun to the nipples on the drawbar around the coupling head mechanism. If the drawbar is covered by a plastic fairing, the nipples will be found under holes in the fairing. Ensure that the plunger attached to the coupling is free to slide in and out.

For many years this was covered by a flexible gaiter which should be free from cracks or splits. If it is split, replace it.

Unless you have a 'dry ball' friction type stabiliser/coupling head such as Al-Ko or Winterhoff, check that the inside of the coupling which fits over the towball on the car is adequately greased, the catch which locks the coupling on to the ball is lubricated, and its spring is effective.

Finally, lubricate the handbrake mechanism and both the axle of the jockey wheel and the winding handle. Wind the jockey wheel right down until the threaded stem drops out of its outer tube, and grease the stem before replacing. Again, these are tasks which would be covered during a workshop annual service.

Replace Damaged Seals

On the body of the caravan, check all seams and joints in the aluminium cladding, particularly at the corners of the caravan and around the skylight. Any mastic sealant which has dried and cracked should be cleaned out with a knife, and a non- hardening, special seam-dresser sealer should be forced in to replace it. This is rather a chore but very necessary. Ideally, all bodywork seams should be scraped clear of dried or flaking filler and be resealed with the correct mastic every three or four years. A dealer's workshop can do this job for you, or supply suitable filler so that you can do it yourself. Few jobs will prolong the life of your caravan more than this important precaution.

A clean caravan body is worth the effort

Clean Bodywork

At the end of a season the caravan could look rather travel-stained, dead insects and black streaks being the main features. A good wash in mild detergent followed by a hose down should cope with the insects. Use a stepladder and floor mop to deal with the roof.

If washing does not move the black streaks, which usually appear under the windows, don't rush in with patent car cleaners. Car paint is usually cellulose while caravan paint is acrylic, and not all preparations are suitable for both. Some car cleaners tend to be mildly abrasive and can ruin the paintwork on a caravan. Personally I use a special creamy caravan cleaner called 'Silky', readily available from accessory shops. This shifts almost any marks and leaves an excellent gloss finish.

There are, however, a number of good branded cleaning and polishing agents available from dealers' accessory shops.

A final word on caravan cleaning. DO NOT be tempted to use a pressure washer on a caravan. It is not designed to withstand such treatment in the way that a saloon car is. A pressure washer carries a real danger of those two words much dreaded in caravanning circles, ie 'water ingress'.

Check Lighting

All road lights on the caravan should be checked. If the washing has left moisture inside the plastic light covers, check the tightness of the holding screws and, if necessary, replace the rubber seals around the lights. Tighten up the screws inside the light fittings, ensuring that an adequate earth connection is made. A small squirt of WD40 in the bulb fitting is worthwhile. At the same time check your 12N and 12S plugs which make the electrical connections between the caravan and car and if they are corroded, replace them. *(This was covered in the 12-volt section, Chapter 6)*. If they are in good condition, treat both, and the sockets on the car, with WD40 lubricant.

Clean and Ventilate Interior

Inside the caravan, ensure that carpets and cushions are cleaned, preferably vacuumed. Stand seat-cushions/mattresses up on edge to ensure a flow of air around them; better still, if you have space available take all movable upholstery indoors for the winter. If fabrics are left in the van, then use a small dehumidifier *(available from any good DIY store)* to gather any moisture. In a 15 foot or larger caravan use two dehumidifiers, one at each end.

You do not want winter visitors

Thoroughly clean out and wash all cupboards and drawers, taking care that no crumbs are left about. *(We had a resident mouse during one winter, which had gained access through a slightly oversized hole in the floor designed to take a water pipe. It must have had a rugged digestive system, for it ate everything it could find - wood, plastic and fabric.)* Believe me, God's little furry creatures you don't need, so don't leave anything to tempt them, and don't leave access for them.

All metal hinges and catches on cupboards and worktops should have a squirt of WD40.

Drain Containers

If you leave your water containers and chemical toilet in the caravan, make sure that all are empty and dry. Leave off or open all screw tops, caps, valves etc. to ensure an adequate fresh air supply. Check all internal water and gas pipe joints for leaks. **Remember that a water heater, either storage or instantaneous type, must be drained against frost damage.**

Battery

Don't forget your faithful servant - the caravan battery. A battery lasts longer if used rather than being left to lie fallow during the winter.

If you can connect your caravan to a 230 volt supply, charge up the battery occasionally, in situ in the caravan, then discharge it partly by switchin on the internal lights or any 12-volt appliance. In other words, use it, then charge it again.

Keep it topped up with deionised water, unless it is one of those no-maintenance jobs, and keep the terminals or battery posts greased with a little Vaseline. It is easy to overlook the battery during the winter, but look after it, give it a bit of use and it will look after you.

Do note that you should not charge your van battery - assuming it is a 'leisure' battery - with the charger you keep in the garage to top up your car battery. The two are incompatible, unless your charger is of the more sophisticated variety which can be switched between 'leisure battery' mode and 'car battery' mode.

Having the caravan occasionally hooked up to mains is also useful since it enables you to run a fan heater inside the van to dispel any suggestion of damp.

Look after your battery in the winter and it will look after you in the summer

Roadworthiness

On the subject of maintenance, let me sound a note of warning.

The caravan press, and the national press, have been featuring reports of roadside caravan checks by traffic police. The results are disturbing. In some instances over 75 per cent of caravans have been found to be unroadworthy, either through physical faults in the caravan - brakes, tyres, suspension, chassis, coupling gear etc - or through badly distributed loads, illegally overloaded, dangerous nose-weights and so on.

The anti-caravan lobby are seizing on these reports to emphasise the fact that a caravan attracts no road tax, is not registered as a vehicle, is not subject to an MOT test and so forth. Maybe they're right, and I am sure the day will come when some of these conditions will have to be met. I am all in favour of an MOT test, but it would be unworkable unless the caravan was registered, complete with separate numberplate, so where does it end? It is up to us.

If you were stopped for a roadside check on your car/caravan outfit, and you were asked:

1. **The kerbside weight of your car.**
2. **The authorised maximum laden weight of your van (or MTPLM).**
3. **The actual nose-weight of the van at the time.**

would you know the answers? This data can easily be gleaned from the van handbooks, and kept in your car, and you should know these details.

Would you take off in an overloaded aircraft? Of course you wouldn't.

The message is clear. Unless you are capable of dismantling and assessing the condition of your caravan wheel bearings and your complete braking and coupling systems, you should have your van professionally serviced at least once a year.

The law has quite rightly clamped down on unroadworthy motor vehicles, and make no mistake, caravans will be next. The more these roadside checks come up with the sort of disturbing figures we have already seen, the sooner the day of reckoning will come.

Caravanners are, in the main, sensible and responsible folk. The least we can do is to ensure that at all times, our caravans are safe for our families to live in and safe to take on the Queen's highway. Remember the definition of good driving and towing? It's a mixture of good manners and common sense. In no way can towing an unroadworthy or overloaded caravan be equated with common sense.

Weatherproof covers

A final offering on the subject of laying up for the winter. We know that the joints or seams in the aluminium outer cladding of your van are sealed with a non-hardening waterproof mastic compound. These joints are usually covered by an extruded alloy strip, often with a coloured plastic insert.

We also know that this mastic compound doesn't last forever. Do you really fancy the idea of your pride and joy standing out there in January, with weeks of incessant rain battering it? I certainly didn't, and I thought of all that water seeking, and possibly finding, any hairline crack in the sealing compound's defences, and creeping heaven knows where inside the laminated walls of the van.

Repair costs to this sort of damage run into telephone numbers, so one winter I bought a plastic cover, with eyelets along the edges. Once over the caravan, one had to mitre or fold the corners, and tie the whole thing down. It wasn't expensive, but I wish I hadn't bothered.

When we took if off in the spring the crackly plastic had naturally moved somewhat, stirred by the wind, and had thoroughly scratched all the windows - and to a lesser extent, some of the paintwork. I did manage to remove the scratches from the windows with hours of hard work and Brasso which, being mildly abrasive, works like certain proprietary brands of car bodywork cleaners.

Nowadays, the definitive answer to the question of caravan covers comes from Yorkshire, in the shape of Specialised Accessories, a company based in Shipley in Yorkshire. They had for some time produced tailor-made covers for classic cars from a revolutionary new fabric. They have now diversified into caravan

Caravanners are generally sane and sensible folk

covers which are quite simply brilliant. In 2003 they won the Practical Caravan award for the best caravan cover.

The fabric meets two essential criteria: *(i)* it is completely waterproof and *(ii)* it incorporates a breathable membrane within its multi-layer construction, thus guarding against the damaging effects of condensation. The laminated spun bond synthetic fabric is soft to the touch, and will not scratch.

The Specialised Accessories cover is not just an oblong piece of fabric with eyelets. It is tailored to fit, and I mean FIT your caravan. When I saw their advertisement in one of the caravan magazines and contacted them, they sent me a comprehensive measurement form to fill in and return, together with details of my make and model of caravan. They also sent a sample of the extremely impressive fabric. Shortly after, I received their quote for a tailor-made cover, specifically to fit the van. The cover arrived with little delay, and Herself and I fitted it on a thankfully wind-free day, after having washed and thoroughly dried the van.

Every cover is individually cut and made for each customer, and we were frankly astonished at the quality of the fit and the workmanship. The cover actually reaches right down to the skirt of the van, and is fastened in place by three or four long ties which pass right underneath the van. In addition they supply extra storm ties which again pass underneath the van and right over the top. They also include a generous piece of spare fabric in the event of your having to effect a repair. This is unlikely as long as you remember to cover, or pad, any sharp protrusion such as the projecting ends of the horizontal rain gutters.

Tailor made covers are worth consideration

An English winter can play havoc with a caravan, despite its build quality, but with a Specialised Accessories cover, it's as good as being in a ventilated garage. There are now no complicated measurement forms to fill in; they have a database of the dimensions and details of almost all current caravans, so placing an order is simple.

Delivery is about three weeks and prices start at around £250 - a very reasonable sum for such an effective piece of equipment. **See *Useful Contacts* at the back of the book.**

Access to the caravan when covered is simple. They provide a flap to give access to the van door, which is sealed around top and side with sturdy Velcro. The door flap on our cover, true to my diagram and measurements, coincided with the van door to the inch.

There is no longer any need to take measurements of your caravan or fill in a complicated form. Specialised Accessories have a computerised database of all modern caravans' dimensions. position of door, antenna, flue etc. Only if ordering for an older van might you need to measure it yourself.

The covers are made from an environmentally friendly shade of green fabric, and our van now stands there behind the garage, snug and weatherproof, looking for all the world like a green dumpling. It is as good as being in a ventilated garage.

It is obviously not cheap, but then neither is bodywork restoration and repair once damp has penetrated. In fact, the cover is incredibly good value for money. If you consider that a good stormproof winter coat, which is both waterproof and breathes, will set you back around £250 including VAT and carriage. For an average 15 foot caravan, and then consider that the cover takes about 50 square metres of fabric per caravan, then the price is indeed very reasonable. Contact Specialised Accessories for a quote - you will be pleasantly surprised **See *Useful Contacts* at the back of the book.**

> An English winter can play havoc with a caravan

Checklist:

Maintenance & Laying Up ✔

1 Rust and damp are the main enemies. Use grease, WD40 and Waxoyl where appropriate. ✔

2 During winter lay-up get the wheels off the ground. Better still, get them off the caravan. ✔

3 Clean the interior meticulously - no crumbs etc ✔

4 Keep the van ventilated. ✔

5 A dehumidifier (or moisture gatherer) is well worthwhile. ✔

6 Leave all filler caps, etc off water containers and toilet. ✔

7 Sterilise water pipes. ✔

8 Drain water heaters against frost. Forget at your peril. ✔

9 Check external seams for dry or loose filler. ✔

10 Leave the fridge door open during lay-up, or indeed whenever it is switched off. ✔

11 Have your van serviced annually by a qualified workshop, testing gas, water and electrical system plus chassis, brakes, couplings etc. To save on this is false economy and potentially dangerous. ✔

12 Reseal all body seams every three or four years. ✔

13 Don't forget the battery. ✔

14 Get a good weatherproof cover. ✔

Caravanning for the Handicapped 13

Caravanning is by no means restricted to the hale and hearty. Many who are confined to wheelchairs, the partially or non-sighted, and a great number of otherwise physically handicapped people have for years, enjoyed the freedom of caravanning.

For many this necessitates some structural modifications to the caravan itself.

Wheelchair-bound caravanners are a particular case and their needs can include a wider entrance door, a ramp, probable modifications to the toilet and the bed, lowering the height of the sink and gas hob, and so on.

There are two firms with great experience of this sort of work. The first is **A1 Leisure** who are based near Darlington, County Durham, and the second is **Fry's Caravans**, who are based at Hutton Cranswick in East Yorkshire. **See** *Useful Contacts* **at the back of the book.**

They have their own body shop, and can undertake modification and construction work which is normally beyond the scope of a caravan dealer.

Both these companies can effect modification to widen doorways, adapt bed and washroom layouts and fit hoists to suit the many and varied needs of disabled and physically handicapped caravanners.

Customs and Excise regulations provide for this type of work, on behalf of the disabled, to be exempt from VAT.

During my caravanning years I have met a number of people with varying degrees of handicap, who were obviously deriving immense pleasure from the freedom that caravanning offers. It is really only financial constraint that limits the extent to which a caravan can be adapted to cater for a handicapped person.

Both the major clubs have the toilet facilities, reception areas etc suitably modified on all their sites, to comply with or exceed the requirements of current legislation for the disabled.

> Many handicapped people enjoy the freedom caravanning brings

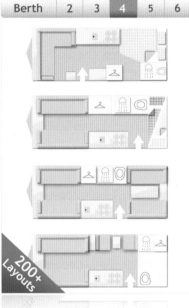
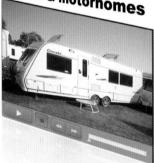

To Sum Up

14

That's about it really. I have tried to avoid being too technical and by no means have I covered the subject comprehensively. The object was to produce a guide to some of the aspects of caravanning and motor homes, which might bewilder a newcomer but which an older hand might also find useful and of interest.

In common with motoring, sailing and photography, to name only a few popular activities, caravanning is something in which you can just as easily dabble or become deeply involved. As with the other three subjects, you can certainly spend a lot of money although this is by no means essential.

Certainly, as with our examples of motoring, sailing and photography, you can get very technical indeed, although this is in no way necessary in order to enjoy the hobby. As a source of technical advice and information, you can always rely on one of the caravanning clubs. They have a wealth of informative leaflets on the many aspects of caravanning and, if there is no leaflet, will gladly supply you with any help or information on your own particular problem. Using a caravan without joining one of the clubs is rather like going to a concert wearing ear plugs. The National Caravan Council also are always willing to give advice and assistance.

Caravan dealers are specialists.

Use them

Finally, of course, who better to turn to than your own local caravan dealer? Caravan and motor home dealers are specialists, with a wealth of technical knowledge and know-how. The great majority strive to build and maintain a reputation for helpfulness and service to the customer.

That's you, so don't be afraid to ask if you need help.

15 And finally...

On the South Cornish coast is a small, rather remote village which we will call Porthfallow. Just outside the village is Arthur's farm. This consists of a cottage with no mains services whatsoever, and a few fields which slope gently down to the cliff top. From there a short path leads down to a rocky beach. The view from the fields is breathtaking, and the peace is indescribable.

We first met Arthur many years ago when our children were small. He has made a comfortable living from families who have camped and caravanned in his fields. At our first meeting Arthur wore a tweed cap and jacket of indeterminable pattern, corduroy trousers and wellies. He wears these same items to this day, in hot or cold weather alike. He doesn't say a lot, he has a simple philosophy and is good company. Both Arthur and his cottage look as though they have been there for about 200 years.

One camps either in the pasture or the 'medder' - not much to choose between them. Each has the same superb view of the cliff top, the sweeping bay and the sea. Each boasts one water tap, and the sanitary essentials are in the pasture. Here Arthur gets a gent with a JCB to dig a pit at the beginning of the season, with back-fill and shovel left handily alongside. Toilets are emptied here and by the end of the summer it's about filled in.

We have caravanned with our young family over the years in Arthur's 'medder' and in sites at home and abroad. These have ranged from the very basic up to sites with swimming pools, bars, discos, take-aways and so on. We have served our time through the trauma of the school holiday travel and crowded roads and ferries, but the youngsters are now all self-supporting, thankfully, and we can please ourselves. We can steal away in June or at the end of September or even both. We have graduated. Caravanning now in our comfortable two-berth. Herself, me and Polly, our retriever, who has got caravanning down to a fine art.

We both love Brittany and the French people, the sunshine and the atmosphere of the well-run continental campsites. To me, though, the essence of caravanning is a weekend at our favourite and mostly deserted location in Derbyshire. Better still in the evening of an Indian summer in early October in Arthur's 'medder' with a glass of ale at hand and the mind in neutral.

15

Children are back at school, all the people in funny hats have gone home, and Porthfallow returns to normal for the rest of the year. (*I'm told that sex and cider constitute the principle recreation in Porthfallow of a winter, and come to that there's not much more to do in the summer.*)

If the bright lights are not for you, then I hope you find your own Porthfallow. I'm certainly not telling you where ours is.

Go safely and enjoy your freedom.

Those were the closing thoughts to an earlier edition, written several years ago, and I wouldn't want to change a word.

Time waits for no man, however, and sadly I have to record that, since then, both Arthur and Polly, the retriever, have passed on. I hope Arthur was admitted through the pearly gates, no doubt still in his ratting jacket and wellies. Polly, who was getting on a bit, will hopefully be dozing in celestial sunshine. We miss them both.

Happily, we have found another site not a million miles away from Arthur's 'medder' - equally tranquil and with better plumbing.

Some years ago I wrote that caravanning leaves one torn between returning to places you know and treasure, and the delight of discovering new ones.

Nothing has changed.

And finally...

Associations

Camping and Caravanning Club,
Greenfields House
Westwood Way
Coventry CV4 8JH
0845 130 7631
Carefree International Travel 0845 130 7701
UK sites booking 0845 130 7701

Caravan Club
East Grinstead House
East Grinstead
West Sussex RH19 1UA
01342 326944
Travel service 01342 316101
UK sites booking 01342 327490

National Caravan Council
Catherine House
Victoria Road
Aldershot
Hampshire GU11 1SS
01252 318251

The Forestry Commission
Forest Holidays
01295 770 532

Royal Society for the Protection of Birds
The Lodge
Sandy
Beds. SG19 2DL
01767 693680

National Park Authorities

Brecon Beacons National Park Authority
Glamorgan Street
Brecon
Powys LD3 7DP

Dartmoor National Park Authority
Haytor Road
Bovey Tracey
Newton Abbot
Devon TQ13 9JQ

Exmoor National Park Authority
Exmoor House
Dulverton
Somerset TA22 9HL

Lake District National Park Authority
County Hall
Kendal
Cumbria LA9 7RL

Northumberland National Park Authority
Bede House
All Saints Centre
Newcastle-upon-Tyne NE1 2DH

North Yorkshire Moors National Park Authority
The Old Vicarage
Bondgate
Helmsley
Yorkshire YO6 5BP

Peak District National Park Authority
Aldern House
Baslow Road
Bakewell
Derbyshire DE4 1AE

Pembrokeshire Coast National Park Authority

County Offices
Haverfordwest SA62 6NW

Snowdonia National Park Authority

Penrhyndeudraeth
Gwynedd LL48 4LS

Yorkshire Dales National Park Authority

Yorebridge House
Bainbridge
Leyburn
North Yorkshire DL8 3EE

Accessories & Services

A1 Leisure

Forge Group House
17 Cleveland Trading Estate
Cleveland Street
Darlington
County Durham DL1 2PB

01325 254791

www.a1leisure.org.uk
Caravan modifications for the disabled

Al-Ko Kober Ltd

Sales 01926 818500

www.al-ko.co.uk
Manufacturers of Caravan Parts and accessories

Ashley Banks Ltd

5 King Street
Langtoft
Peterborough PE6 9NF

01778 560651
Caravan air conditiong units

Belling Appliances Ltd

Talbot Road
Mexborough
South Yorkshire S64 8AJ

01709 579902

`Malaga' water and Belling space heaters

Bulldog Security Products

Stretton Road
Much Wenlock
Shropshire TF13 6DH

01952 728171

Caravan security equipment

Calor Gas Ltd

Athena Drive
Tachbrook Park
Warwick CV34 6RL

0800 626626

(or see telephone directory for local depot)
Suppliers of LPG

Camping Cheque UK

Hotline Offers 0870 405 4057

www.campingcheque.co.uk
Continental 4- & 5-star camp site discount vouchers

Caravan Mover Installations

Park Lane
Dove Valley Park
South Derbyshire DE65 5BG

0800 389 4648
'Kwikee' hydraulic caravan levelling system

Caravan Finder Ltd

01394 388 334

sales@caravanfinder.co.uk
Website for sale or purchase of caravans

Caravan Storage Site Owners Assn (CaSSOA)

Market Square House
St. James Street
Nottingham NG1 6SG

0115 934 9826
Secure storage sites

Accessories & Services (Cont'd)

Carver & Co (Engineers) Ltd
For all Carver enquiries contact Truma (UK)
Space heaters, water heaters, pump systems and Caravan Mover

CRiS - see Equifax Europe

Dometic Ltd
99 Oakley Road
Luton, Beds LU4 9GE
01582 494111
www.dometic.co.uk
Formerly Electrolux Products

Equifax Europe UK
25 Chapel Street
London NW1 5DS
01722 411430
Holders of the CRiS database

Fry's Caravans
Cranswick Industrial Estate
Beverley Road
Hutton Cranswick
Driffield
East Yorkshire YO25 9QE
01377 271383
www.frys.co.uk
Caravan modification for the disabled

Gaslow International Ltd
Manor House Stables
Normanton on Soar
Leicestershire LE12 5HB
01509 843331
www.gaslow.co.uk
LPG regulators & gas safety systems

Grade (UK) Ltd

3 Central Court
Finch Close
Lenton Industrial Estate
Nottingham NG7 2NN

0115 986 7151

Omnidirectional TV aerials

Grove Products Ltd

Broadway, Hyde
Cheshire SK14 4QF

0161 367 7171

sales@groveproducts.co.uk

Wholesalers of wide range of caravan accessories

Hella Ltd

Wildmere Industrial Estate, Banbury
Oxon OX16 7JU

01295 272233

Electrical supplies and towing kits

Mr Shifta

0115 973 1335

www.shifta.com

Electric caravan mover

Mobile Homes Insurance Service

4 Augusta Place, Leamington Spa
Warwicks, CV32 5EL

01926 452626

Caravan Insurers

Munster Simms Engineering Ltd

Old Belfast Road
Bangor BT19 1LT
N. Ireland

01247 270531

`Whale' water supply systems

Accessories & Services (Cont'd)

Powrwheel Ltd

6 Priory Industrial Estate
Airspeed Road, Christchurch
Dorset BH23 4HD

01425 283 293

www.powrwheel.com
Remote controlled electric caravan mover

Safe and Secure Products

Chestnut House, Chesley Hill
Wick, Bristol BS15 5NE

0117 9374747 or 9374494

Security equipment – locks, alarms and wheel clamps

Sunnflair Ltd

Cutlers Road
South Woodham Ferrers
Chelmsford
Essex CM3 5XJ

01245 329933

Sunncamp lightweight porch awnings

Specialised Accessories

Riverdale House
Dockfield Road
Shipley
West Yorks BD11 7AD

01943 864828

Weatherproof caravan covers

Thetford Ltd

Centrovell Industrial Estate
Caldwell Road
Nuneaton
Warwicks CV11 4UD

01203 322700

Portable and fitted toilets

Touring Cheque

08703 667808

www.touringcheque.co.uk
European 4 and 5 star site discount vouchers

Truma (UK)

Beeches Park
Eastern Avenue
Burton on Trent
DE13 0BB

01283 586050

www.truma.com
Truma and Carver caravan heating equipment
All Carver sales enquiries

Towsafe/HPI

Dolphin House
New Street
Salisbury
Wiltshire SP1 2TB

01722 413 434
Safe car/caravan matching scheme

Witter Towbars

18 Canal Side
Chester CH1 3LL

01244 284500

www.witter-towbards.co.uk
Towbars

W4 Ltd

Ford Lane Industrial Estate
Arundel
West Sussex BN18 0DF

01243 553355
Mains tester plugs – caravan accessories